About the author . . .

Robert B. Nelson is an established business author and vice president of product development for Blanchard Training and Development, Inc., a leading human resources development company located in San Diego, California. He is the author of several books, including *Decision Point* (1992) and *We Have to Start Meeting Like This* (1989).

Jennifer Wallick is a computer scientist for HNC Inc., a high-tech software development company. She frequently makes and helps others with presentations and has written articles for a number of journals.

THE PRESENTATION PRIMER

Getting Your Point Across

The *Briefcase Books* Series

Managing Stress: Keeping Calm Under Fire
Barbara J. Braham

Business Negotiating Basics
Peter Economy

Straight Answers to People Problems
Fred E. Jandt

Empowering Employees through Delegation
Robert B. Nelson

The Presentation Primer: Getting Your Point Across
Robert B. Nelson

Jennifer Wallick

Listen for Success: A Guide to Effective Listening
Arthur K. Robertson

THE
PRESENTATION
PRIMER
Getting Your Point Across

Robert B. Nelson

Jennifer B. Wallick

Professional Publishing

Burr Ridge, IL 60521
New York, NY 10001

This publication is designed to provide accurate and authoritative information in regard to the subject matter covered. It is sold with the understanding that neither the author or the publisher is engaged in rendering legal, accounting, or other professional service. If legal advice or other expert assistance is required, the services of a competent professional person should be sought.

From a Declaration of Principles jointly adopted by a Committee of the American Bar Association and a Committee of Publishers.

Senior sponsoring editor:	Cynthia A. Zigmund
Project editor:	Beth Yates
Production manager:	Laurie Kersch
Designer:	Larry J. Cope
Art coordinator:	Heather Burbridge
Compositor:	Wm. C. Brown Communications, Inc.
Typeface:	11/13 Palatino
Printer:	Book Press, Inc.

Library of Congress Cataloging-in-Publication Data

Nelson, Robert B.
   The presentation primer : getting your point across / Robert B. Nelson, Jennifer B. Wallick.
     p.   cm. — (The Briefcase books series)
   Includes index.
   ISBN 1-55623-846-0   0-7863-0200-3 (Paperback)
   1. Business presentations. 2. Public speaking. I. Wallick, Jennifer B. II. Title. III. Series.
HF5718.22.N45   1994
808.5'1—dc20   93–29855

Printed in the United States of America
1 2 3 4 5 6 7 8 9 0 BP 0 9 8 7 6 5 4 3

The Briefcase Books Series

Research shows that people who buy business books (1) want books that can be read quickly, perhaps on a plane trip, commuting on a train, or overnight, and (2) feel their time and money were well spent if they get two or three useful insights or techniques for improving their professional skills or helping them with a current problem at work.

Briefcase Books were designed to meet these two criteria. They focus on necessary skills and problem areas, and include real-world examples from practicing managers and professionals. Inside these books you'll find useful, practical information and techniques in a straightforward, concise, and easy-to-read format.

This book and others like it in the Briefcase Books series can quickly give you insights and answers regarding your current needs and problems. And they are useful references for future situations and problems.

If you find this book or any other in this series to be of value, please share it with your co-workers. With tens of thousands of new books published each year, any book that can simplify the growing complexities in managing others needs to be circulated as widely as possible.

Robert B. Nelson
Series Editor

Foreword

My mission in life has been to be a conveyor of simple truths. It is for that reason that I'm pleased to be able to introduce the Briefcase Books series, which seeks to provide simple, practical, and direct answers to the most common problems managers face on a daily basis.

It has been my experience that in the field of business common sense is not common practice. So it is refreshing to find a series of books that glorifies common sense in dealing with people in the workplace.

Take the skill of listening. We all know that it is important to listen, yet how many of us actually do it well? I suggest it would be rare to find one in a hundred managers that is truly a good listener. Most people focus on what they are going to say next when someone else is talking. They would seldom if ever think to check what they thought they heard to make sure it is accurate. And they seldom acknowledge or attempt to deal with emotions when they occur in speaking with someone at work. These are basic errors in the use of this basic skill. And regardless of how much education or experience you have, you should know how to listen.

But how much training have you had on the topic of listening? Have you ever had a course on the topic? Have you ever tested your ability to listen? Have you ever discussed with others how you could listen better with greater comprehension and respect? Probably not. Even though this fundamental interpersonal skill could cripple the most talented individual if he or she is not good at it.

Fortunately, listening is just one of the fundamental skills singled out for its own volume in the Briefcase Books series. Others include books on making presentations, negotiating, problem solving, and handling stress. And other volumes are planned even as I write this.

The Briefcase Books series focuses on those basic skills that managers must master to excel at work. Whether you are new to managing or are a seasoned manager, you'll find these books of value in obtaining useful insights and fundamental knowledge you can use for your entire career.

Ken Blanchard
Co-author
The One Minute Manager

Preface

Sooner or later in your career you will have the opportunity to give a presentation. The presentation may be to co-workers in your department, it may be to a committee or management group, it may be to a professional association, it may be to a civic organization. If you excel in the presentation, you will be effective at communicating your point of view and persuasive in convincing others to accept your course of action. You will experience a sense of accomplishment and euphoria. You will have effectively achieved a wider circle of influence with a larger group of people. In short, you will have a new skill that can help you advance in your chosen field.

Making an effective presentation is a direct result of your planning, preparation, and practice. This book will show you how, in a step-by-step manner, to develop a presentation that achieves the results you want. It takes the mystery out of the process so that you can more easily present powerful, persuasive speeches in your future presentations.

Robert B. Nelson
Jennifer B. Wallick

Contents

Chapter One

So You're Giving a Presentation . . .

WHY PRESENTATIONS ARE IMPORTANT

Your ability to give oral presentations is your key to new opportunities in your life. You will face more and more opportunities to speak to groups as you move into positions of increased responsibility and expertise. Speaking to groups will be an integral part of your job if you ever plan to manage, lead, sell or promote. Each speaking situation is an opportunity for you to display your expertise and to win others over to your way of thinking. It is an important skill worth mastering for many reasons.

Visibility in your organization. Consider your career in an organization. Rising to the top depends on the right type of visibility with the right people. People need to know who you are and what you do—and oral presentations give you the perfect opportunity to present your work and your professional skills. It is much easier for your manager to get your promotion approved when his or her manager knows who you are and what a great job you do. Presentations give you direct access to the managers of an organization and enable you to leave a favorable impression in a short amount of time. It is an established fact of life in organizations that those who present well move well.

A leadership skill. If you want to develop your potential as a leader, you need a clear and powerful speaking style to motivate and inspire others. You need to be able to present the views of others as well as you present your own—to be a spokesperson for a given cause. Your ability to give effective presentations enables you to be an effective leader.

A decision-making tool. A common problem that organizations share is inaccurate communication within the organization. Organizations need people who can clearly communicate information. A clear presentation keeps people in your organization well informed and helps your organization make correct decisions. You are obligated as an employee to make your ideas and recommendations clear and their consequences understandable.

These are a few of the reasons why effective communication is important to master. They add up to more than just getting through the presentation you have been asked to give. These reasons suggest that your ability to present can be one of your most powerful professional skills.

COMMON MYTHS ABOUT PRESENTATIONAL SPEAKING

If you are like most people, your mental image of public speaking has come from years of watching movies and listening to politicians give their campaign speeches. Following are some of the most common misconceptions about presentational speaking.

Myth: Speakers Are Born, Not Made

Don't abandon hope for improving your own speaking skills when you see an accomplished speaker give an inspiring and polished presentation. These speakers—politicians,

Even the best speakers need to prepare for and practice their presentations.

military personnel, church leaders, and so on—are so skilled that it seems as though they have an innate ability to communicate. This is seldom the case. Experienced presenters make public speaking *look* easy. What you probably don't realize is that they are experts on their topics and have given the same presentation several times before. In the beginning they probably shared your fears and doubts but have overcome them with preparation, practice, and experience.

Myth: You Should Copy Someone Else's Speaking Style

Hearing a speaking style that is unique and effective can be misleading for a novice speaker. First, you may be tempted to try to imitate or adopt the style in your own speeches. This seldom works, and when someone else's style is incorporated into your own, your speech usually comes off as insincere and unbelievable. Second, a speaking style that is entertaining and has a lot flare may be very dramatic, but most of the time this kind of speech is not very effective in day-to-day business communications. Presentational speaking focuses on relaying essential information in a clear and effective manner. Very few business presentations, if any, will ever go down in history as memorable speeches, so the role model of a great public figure may not be the best model to adopt for your own speaking style.

Myth: You Never Overcome Stage Fright

There is a common notion that once you have stage fright, it will plague you the rest of your life in any and all speaking situations. This belief helps to reinforce the "why bother to try" attitude about presentational speaking. The fact is that even though experienced public speakers feel stage fright, these individuals learn to use their anxiety to their advantage. They learn to reduce their symptoms to a manageable level and then channel their anxious energy into enthusiasm that improves their presentation. Many experts agree that experiencing nervousness prior to a presentation can be advantageous for the speaker as well as the speaking situation. A speaker who is nervous about speaking is more likely to go to extra lengths to prepare, practice, and double-check all arrangements. The speech is likely to be more dynamic and exciting because the speaker seems more alive. A speaker who isn't nervous often comes across as boring or uninterested. Experts agree that anxiety in speaking situations usually stems from a speaker's wanting to do the best job possible, rather than his or her fearing the situation. Chances are good that you will always have some degree of performance anxiety as you strive toward more and more challenging opportunities. Keep in mind that relief comes from knowing that your goal is not to rid yourself of this anxiety, but to learn to become comfortable with the feeling and to use it to enhance your personal speaking style.

Myth: Manuscript Speaking Is Better

Our role models for speech delivery—TV newscasters, inaugural speeches, conference papers—all read from prepared manuscripts. Although this may be a traditional mode of delivery for certain public presentations, it is not an acceptable mode of delivery for most business presentations. Manuscript speaking is an ineffective crutch for a new speaker that should be avoided at all costs. Because you are reading to the audience rather than communicating with it, you will smother your natural style and put your audience to sleep. Manuscript speaking has the potential of being insulting as well as ineffective for relaying information.

Myth: Presentations Must Be Memorized to Be Effective

Memorization usually wastes preparation time and impedes delivery of your speech. You lose sight of the forest for the trees because you concentrate too much on what specific word comes next. Memorization also makes it hard to recover if you forget a particular word or sentence during delivery of your presentation. Instead, the modern-day speaker should work from a few notes that outline the presentation. The delivery should be natural, as in a discussion. The main idea and points to be communicated should be learned or memorized, but the exact wording and delivery can vary with the specific occasion.

Myth: Presentations Must Be Formal to Be Effective

Often we conclude that a speech should be formal because we do not know the audience very well or because the audience includes important managers and decision makers. This myth is a problem because if your personal style is not a formal one, you will not feel at ease in the speaking situation. You will try to be something or someone you are not and your delivery will feel and look awkward. Besides, more formal often means more boring. Stale, lofty language coupled with a dry, monotonous tone are common characteristics of a formal delivery.

Informal presentations that are well organized are much more effective for several reasons. First, they are more interesting to listen to. An informal style allows the audience to feel closer to the speaker. Second, an informal delivery style allows speakers to be themselves. You are more persuasive and sincere when you are comfortable delivering your speech.

WHAT YOU WILL LEARN FROM THIS BOOK

This book teaches you how to prepare and deliver an effective business presentation—whether the presentation is for 5 or 500 people. This book uses three simple principles to turn you into an effective presenter.

One: Understand, Control, and Use Your Stage Fright

The first step in preparing a good presentation is to understand your stage fright so that it does not become a roadblock to preparing your presentation. Chapter 2 explores

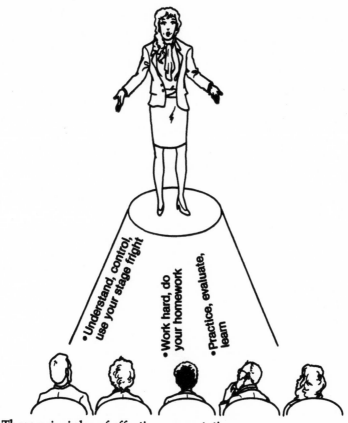

Three principles of effective presentations.

where your stage fright comes from and gives you a variety of techniques for controlling your symptoms of stage fright.

Two: Work Hard and Do Your Homework

Given the proper instruction, attitude, and preparation, almost everyone can become an excellent speaker. The magic surrounding your presentation as well as your apprehension about it will fade as the reality of the task becomes clear. The reality of delivering a quality presentation is a logical, step-by-step approach for preparing and practicing your presentation. Chapters 3 through 5 give you a step-by-step formula for deciding what you want to say and determining how you want to say it. Chapter 9 gives some suggestions for special types of speaking situations (such as how to deal with a hostile audience).

Three: Practice, Evaluate, and Learn

To deliver a good presentation, you need to practice and you need to evaluate your performance each time you practice. Chapters 6 through 8 walk you through practicing and evaluating your practices. Chapter 10 helps you learn from your experience and identify ways to improve your next presentation.

EVALUATING YOUR CURRENT SKILLS

Research shows that any learning experience is more successful when you have preconceived ideas about what you want to learn. This book will help you more if you know what specific areas you need to improve. Following are two preliminary surveys. The first helps you to take inventory of your present speaking skills and decide what you would like to accomplish. The second allows you to compare your self-perceptions with the qualities of a good public speaker.

TAKE YOUR SPEAKING INVENTORY

Self-description. Describe yourself as a speaker by selecting five descriptive words that come to mind (for example, humorous, boring):

1. _____

2. _____

3. _____

4. _____

5. _____

Strengths. List the characteristics that are your greatest assets in presentational speaking: _____

_____

_____

_____

_____

_____

_____

Weaknesses. List those areas that you have to improve to be better at presentational speaking: _____

_____

_____

_____

_____

_____

Behavioral goal. Describe how you would imagine yourself if you were effective at presentational speaking:

_____

_____

_____

_____

_____

Knowledge goal. List several specific questions that you would like answered before you have finished this book:

_____

_____

_____

_____

Commitment to learning. How do you specifically stand to benefit by becoming more effective at presentational speaking?

_____

_____

_____

_____

_____

SCORE YOURSELF AS A SPEAKER

Read each question and circle the letter that best represents your present status as a public speaker. This is just your own estimate of yourself and not a scientific test. Tally your score to find out how your characteristics rank against the characteristics of an accomplished public speaker.

1. When called upon unexpectedly to speak, what do I do?
    A. Get confused.
    B. Keep cool and collected.
    C. Get major symptoms of stage fright such as heart palpitations and stuttering.
    D. Get minor symptoms of stage fright such as a dry mouth.
    E. Think well on my feet.
2. What is my attitude while speaking?
    A. Worried
    B. Earnestly interested
    C. Continuously enthusiastic
    D. Self-confident
3. Which of the following topics do have I the most information about to give a speech?
    A. My occupation
    B. My hobby
    C. My reading
    D. Personal experiences
    E. Current affairs
4. What effect does my speaking have on the audience?
    A. Usually boring
    B. Tolerated
    C. Persuasive
    D. Convincing

E. Entertaining

F. Instructive

5. What do I do to prepare for a speech?

   A. Gather and arrange ample material.

   B. Rely on inspiration from the occasion.

   C. Jot down a few ideas.

6. My memory of speech points is

   A. Poor

   B. Fair

   C. Good

   D. Excellent

7. In opening a talk, what do I do?

   A. Apologize

   B. Hem and haw

   C. Quickly catch favorable attention

8. My speeches

   A. Have a pleasing closing.

   B. Fizzle out and stop.

   C. Result in favorable action by the audience.

9. How is my platform presence?

   A. Slouchy

   B. Composed

   C. Ill at ease

10. How is my vocabulary?

    A. Too meager

    B. Ordinary

    C. Complete and accurate

11. How is my enunciation?

    A. Clear

    B. Mumbled or slurred

    C. Restrained behind tight lips

12. How do my ideas come out?
    A. Logically arranged
    B. Jumbled
    C. Fairly clear
    D. Psychologically effective
13. When speaking, I think chiefly
    A. Of myself.
    B. Of the audience.
    C. Of the words of my speech.
14. How keen is my desire to speak in public?
    A. I would rather have this ability than any other.
    B. I wish I had the gift.
    C. I would study half an hour daily for four
       months.

To score your public speaking efficiency, add the figures
assigned to each question. High score is 100; low score is 10.

   1. A(0), B(2), C(6), D(0), E(8)
   2. A(1), B(6), C(8), D(5)
   3. A(5), B(5), C(5), D(5), E(5)
   4. A(0), B(1), C(8), D(6), E(8), F(5)
   5. A(8), B(0), C(3)
   6. A(0), B(1), C(5), D(3)
   7. A(1), B(0), C(8)
   8. A(4), B(1), C(8)
   9. A(0), B(5), C(1)
  10. A(0), B(2), C(6)
  11. A(8), B(0), C(1)
  12. A(6), B(0), C(4), D(9)
  13. A(1), B(6), C(3)
  14. A(8), B(2), C(4)

Chapter Two

Overcoming Your Stage Fright

Stage fright is addressed early in this book so that it doesn't haunt you during each step of your preparation. We focus first on understanding your stage fright and then on overcoming, controlling, and utilizing your anxiety to your advantage.

UNDERSTANDING STAGE FRIGHT

Most speech counselors and instructors believe that stage fright stems from the prehistoric defense system of the human species. When an early human was faced with a perceived threat, the physical reaction was that of fleeing or fighting, and energy was directed toward one of those two ends. As we are faced with perceived threats in our modern world, we have the same reaction. Unfortunately, neither fleeing nor fighting is an appropriate reaction in the business setting. We are left with an increased level of energy with only a few avenues for using it. If we don't direct this extra energy through the proper channels, our extra energy will ooze out in inappropriate and distracting ways.

Let's consider several aspects of stage fright and unravel some of the mysteries behind it.

Stage fright stems from our prehistoric defense systems.

Stage Fright Is Normal

Stage fright is your body's way of alerting you to be prepared. The more important the situation is to you, the more stage fright you will experience. If you don't feel anxious about the presentation, then you probably won't have much energy or enthusiasm. You won't prepare as well and you won't feel as excited about it. Speakers who aren't anxious about their presentation run the risk of being inappropriate, offending the audience, using humor in bad taste, or rambling on—oblivious to the audience's reaction. Stage fright can have a positive effect on your public speaking. You are much worse off if you aren't fearful of the situation. Be glad you are anxious about your presentation and learn to use your anxiety to your advantage.

Stage Fright Seems More Severe to the Speaker

When you are on stage, your symptoms of stage fright are amplified, especially when you are looking for them. Very few of your stage fright symptoms can be detected by audience members, and symptoms that are detectable rarely detract from your presentation. An important point to remember is that almost everyone in the audience understands stage fright and will overlook its symptoms. Unfortunately, what usually happens is that, for example, a speaker will notice his or her voice cracking and believe that it is noticeable to the audience. This will make the speaker more uneasy, causing new symptoms of stage fright to appear. This cycle can escalate to the point where the speaker feels that he or she cannot continue. Members of the audience probably didn't think twice when the speaker's voice first cracked. It was the speaker who escalated a small symptom of stage fright into a major problem.

Stage Fright Escalates the More You Seek to Escape It

One of the ironies of stage fright is that the more you try to avoid it, the more you are likely to experience it. People often come to fear the feeling of fear itself. Instead of trying to hide from fear in a speaking situation, you need to become comfortable with being uncomfortable. You need to accept that your fear is legitimate and be confident that it will quickly pass. You need to ignore negative symptoms and seek positive reinforcement from yourself or from others. You must make a truce with fear rather than fight a battle you cannot win.

Stage fright symptoms seem more severe to the speaker.

CONQUERING STAGE FRIGHT

Start by taking a positive and aggressive attitude about speaking. The first moment that you are asked to give a presentation, respond with, "I'd be honored." Keep in mind that a confident, aggressive approach to presentational speaking keeps most imagined fears from becoming a reality. Next, take the time to prepare for your presentation. Some experts suggest that as much as 75 percent of speech anxiety can be avoided through adequate preparation.

Making the time to prepare for your presentation may be easier said than done, but it is worth it. You will feel more comfortable and confident when you deliver a well-prepared speech. Let's look at some specific approaches for overcoming stage fright. Different techniques will work for different people.

Aware—Accept—Act

This technique uses a simple three-step formula to cope with your stage fright.

Become aware. Be aware of what is happening to you when you are fearful. Once you are sensitized to your fear, it is easier for you to stop your fear from escalating. Even panic, which occurs without warning, can be curtailed when you recognize what is happening to you. Pay attention to physical symptoms such as your breathing pattern and your muscle tension. Your body tells you how nervous or relaxed you feel.

Accept the emotion. Accept fear as being valid, and don't feel guilty or foolish or inferior because of it. To insist that it should not be happening to you is going to make you more fearful. Instead, when fear comes, welcome it. Consider it a form of energy that can motivate you to better prepare prior to a presentation and make you a more enthusiastic speaker during your presentation.

Act on it. After you become aware of and accept fear, you need to act on it. Do something different. Do not become a passive recipient of a feeling you dread. If you don't know what to do to curb your fear, try *any* different behavior. With some experience, you will be able to identify more specifically what action curtails your fear.

Rational Emotive Theory

Rational emotive theory, first developed by Robert Ellis, states that you can control your emotions, including fear and anxiety, through your thoughts. The crux of theory is that you can deliver a winning presentation by thinking through the situation ahead of time. Take the following steps to use the rational emotive theory to deal with your fear of speaking.

Imagine the worst scenario. Imagine the worst thing that can happen to you in your speaking situation. Take your analysis to an extreme. Perhaps the audience might criticize you, or maybe they'll laugh at you. Or maybe they will be so disgusted by your delivery that they will start to ignore you and leave the room. Your manager might become so outraged that he fires you—in front of the group! You might become so stressed that you have a heart attack and die on the spot!

Estimate the chances of its happening. Now, of all the negative consequences that can occur as a result of your presentation, what are the chances that any or all of them will actually materialize? When you really think about it, the chances of any of the negative consequences really happening are usually very small.

Picture what is likely to happen. Now, with the worst case scenarios out of the picture, imagine what is more likely to occur in your speaking situation and what specific problems might realistically arise. Think about some of the tough questions people might ask you. What if you can't answer a question? What if your voice cracks? What if you can't remember what you were going to say?

Minimize potential problems. Decide what you can do minimize the chances of not being able to handle specific problems that are likely to come up. Resolve not to worry about those aspects of the situation which you don't have any control over.

This theory helps change blind fear into a tangible, rational process that can be examined and discussed. When you do this, the mystery of the unknown disappears, and your energy can be directed towards actions that will do the most good.

Systematic Desensitization

Systematic desensitization also uses your imagination to confront both the fear and the situation of speaking. It has proven to be one of the most effective methods for helping people who experience extreme anxiety about presentational speaking. With this method you shut your eyes and attempt to walk through the stressful situation from its earliest conception to its final completion. Whenever you feel stress, you stop the exercise and attempt it again at a later time. No analysis is made as to why the fear exists or why it goes away. You repeat this exercise until you can enact the entire speaking situation and associated behavior, such as the speech preparation, without experiencing physical anxiety.

A different approach that uses the same theory is to practice controlling your fright in situations where you know that no physical harm can come to you. A good example is watching a scary movie. You know that the threat is imagined, yet the symptoms you experience are very real. A scary movie serves as an ideal situation to analyze and practice controlling your fear.

Go to a scary movie, and as you are watching, become aware of what your body is doing. Is your body squirming? Sit erect and face the screen full front. Is your heart pounding? Close your eyes and consciously take longer and deeper breaths. Continue breathing in this deliberate manner as you watch. Experiment with giving yourself suggestions. "This music is not that scary." "This is only a movie." "I am completely relaxed." "The music is scarier than the visual." Find out which suggestions are the most effective in diminishing your symptoms of fear, and remember them so that you can use them in your nightmares of public speaking.

Try going to a scary movie and notice what symptoms of fear you feel. What can you do to reduce or control those symptoms?

By doing this type of exercise, you learn how to control irrational feelings in a rational way. You use your ability to think to overpower your emotions when they are not serving constructive purposes. Establish the point at which fear becomes counterproductive for you if left unchecked. Learn how to contain or diminish that fear.

Hypnosis

The method of hypnosis uses visual imagery to identify what you fear in a speaking situation. You and your hypnotist design suggestions to help you at the specific moment of anxiety. These suggestions are positive statements that boost your confidence or remind you of alternatives that are available to you when you become anxious. With repetition over several weeks, you will be able to integrate the suggestions into your mental and behavioral responses to speaking situations. Hypnosis is possible without the aid of a hypnotist. There are several books available on the topic of self-hypnosis, such as *Self Hypnotism: The Technique and Its Use in Daily Living* (Englewood Cliffs, NJ: Prentice Hall, 1964).

These methods—aware-accept-act, rational emotive theory, systematic desensitization, and hypnosis—represent the most effective techniques known for overcoming stage fright in presentational speaking situations. By using these techniques, you become skilled at managing your level of anxiety and redirecting the normal surge of energy that comes with speaking situations into channels that enhance rather than detract from your presentation.

HANDLING SPECIFIC SYMPTOMS OF STAGE FRIGHT

When you are delivering a presentation, you may find yourself displaying various symptoms of anxiety. Here are some techniques that you can have in your hip pocket in the event of an anxiety attack before or during your presentation. Knowing that you have alternatives such as these will enable you to feel more confident and prepared.

Speechlessness

Warm up your voice before entering the speaking environment, or hum to yourself while you are waiting to start. Repeat the first words of your presentation to yourself. If you become speechless in the middle of your talk, stop and accept the feeling, take a breath, and then begin again. Focus on the face of a friend in the audience and imagine that you are talking to that one person.

"Aaahs" and "Ummmms"

Possibly one of the most difficult mannerisms to correct is the verbal crutch of saying "ah" during a pause in your speech. When excessive, this habit can distract an audience. Practice speaking more deliberately, with intentional pauses, always thinking before you speak. Listen to the sound of your own voice and be aware when your language is becoming sloppy. This trait is usually found with hesitant speakers who are unsure of exactly what they want to say. It usually diminishes with practice.

Blanking Out

Sometimes you might forget what you were going to say. Have a strategy ready in case you blank out during your presentation. Following are some specific techniques that you can adapt to your own style and use as needed.

Acknowledge you forgot. As in a conversation, say, "That point momentarily escapes me," and continue on, "but let's look at the other reasons why . . ."

Fill in the gap. Summarize, repeat the last point, restate your thesis, give a personal example. These will all give you time to remember where you were.

Shift the attention. Ask for questions, poll the group on their opinion or an alternative for what to do next, or take a five-minute break. Remember that no one knows the agenda for your presentation except you.

Refer to your notes. As unobtrusively as possible, glance at your next point. Feel comfortable with a moment or two of silence. Use the silence as a means to emphasize your next point.

Summarize and stop. If you are close to the end of your talk, this can be a good alternative.

Have a catchall. Keep a line ready that makes you feel comfortable regardless of the situation. "It seems like I'm getting ahead of myself. Let me take a second and catch my breath."

Racing

If you find yourself talking faster and faster, pause a moment so that you can gain control of your speed. If you heart is pounding and your head is swimming, pause, close your eyes, and take a deep breath. Try to limit the stimuli that are overexciting you. Imagine a peaceful scene or a calm situation such as working on a favorite pastime. Try using reminders in the margin of your notes, such as "SLOW DOWN," or arrange to have an audience member give you a signal if you begin to talk too fast. Practice pauses so that you are comfortable with silence, and be especially sure that you deliver your key points, such as the introduction, transitions, and closing, more loudly and more slowly.

Stiff or Shaky Muscles

Learn to identify exactly which muscles tense up. Before the presentation, walk around and shake off the extra energy in the tense muscles (particularly in the case of those telltale hands). It also helps to tense and then relax your muscles before the presentation. During the presentation, try to move the muscles that are tense. For example, a stiff front torso can be relaxed by bending at the waist, perhaps to pick up an object, to "break" the rigid body armor. If you have problems with shaky muscles, do not let your presentation make your shaking more apparent. For example, if your hands shake, do not hold up any visual aids or point to items on a board. Likewise, if your knees shake, you may want to start speaking while leaning against the edge of a table. Do not feel locked into having to speak from one specific location, even if a podium is present.

Shortness of Breath

Shortness of breath is caused by excessive muscle tension around your chest and stomach regions. Stretching your arms and taking deep breaths before your presentation help break the chest tension. If you find you are short of breath during a presentation, simply stop and take a deep breath. Take a moment between sentences or phrases to catch your breath and reestablish a natural speaking rhythm. During your pause, take time to think about what you want to say next. Your audience will not mind your pausing for a deep breath. If you feel uncomfortable stopping, give your audience a disclaimer, such as, "Let me take a second to catch my breath. I'm starting to get ahead of myself." Most likely, this will make you come across as being very excited about your topic.

Excessive Perspiration

Getting flushed or warm because of anxiety often makes people sweat excessively. Perspiration is usually beyond your control. The less you worry about it, the less severe the problem will be. You can minimize embarrassment by planning ahead. Have a handkerchief available, and don't be shy about mopping your brow. Your audience will understand; after all, aren't you working very hard on their behalf? Loosen your tight-fitting collar prior to speaking, and, if you wear glasses, dab some cornstarch on the nose bridge to avoid slippage. Wear a white shirt or blouse if you are prone to wet underarms, or simply avoid removing your jacket. You can usually make sure that a glass of water is near the lectern before you begin to speak.

Dry Mouth

Cottonmouth can be uncomfortable, and it affects your ability to pronounce words and speak clearly. If you are prone to this symptom, have a glass of water handy.

Pounding Heart

This symptom is your body's way of preparing you for quick defensive action. The pounding sound in your ears can be distracting, but it cannot be heard by anyone else. Take long, slow breaths before and during the presentation to help slow your heart down. In extreme cases, holding a long, deep breath will help by decreasing the amount of oxygen in your blood.

Cracking Voice

Excessive tension can show quickly in your voice. It usually comes from having tense neck muscles or an inadequate air supply to support your voice. Stretch your neck, clear your throat, and take a deep breath to counteract the effects of this symptom. Pause a moment and have a sip of water.

Shifting or Rocking Body Movements

Excessive body movements are another outlet for nervous energy. Any type of idiosyncratic mannerism will distract from your communication and should be avoided. Before you can conquer these motions, you must first be aware of what they are. Have a friend watch for them during a practice presentation. Keep practicing your presentation with your friend until you have eliminated them.

Loose Change

Hands in the pockets can be annoying to an audience if you are playing with change or keys. It also restricts the use of arm gestures and thus is likely to make your presentation less effective. Try standing with one arm bent in front of you and the other arm at your side. If you do have a tendency to slip a hand into your pocket, use a change purse or be sure that the pocket you slip your hand into is empty.

With the techniques described in this chapter, you are now equipped with the most effective methods known for overcoming, controlling, and redirecting stage fright in presentational speaking situations. By learning and practicing these techniques you will become skilled at managing your level of anxiety and redirecting nervous energy into channels that enhance rather than detract from your presentation. Arm gestures, body movements, and vocal enthusiasm can become the acceptable outlets for your energy and will also serve to enhance your presentational style and effectiveness.

Chapter Three

Planning Your Presentation

When you deliver your presentation, you will be glad for every minute you spent planning it. Planning your presentation doesn't mean coming up with an outline for your presentation—that comes in the next chapter on preparing your presentation. Planning your presentation means that you need to take these steps:

- Decide *what* the purpose of your presentation is.
- Analyze *who* your audience is.
- Think about *where* you will be giving your presentation.

Following are two reasons why assessing your speaking situation ahead of time is so important.

EXAMPLE 1: PLANNING LETS YOU KNOW WHAT TO EXPECT

Planning your presentation helps you know what to expect when you deliver your presentation. Consider the following story of a marketing director in Cleveland, Ohio:

Several years ago the marketing director of a large insurance brokerage firm was asked to present the municipal council her company's competitive bid for a group benefits

Planning your presentation.

contract for employees. She accepted readily. The opportunity was not only flattering but also critical to her professional progress. Visions of a closed deal danced through her head. But when she arrived at the meeting hall, she discovered that the council was holding an open meeting. Along with its members were almost 100 interested local citizens and municipal employees. Panic stricken, she begged off and refused to present her case. She could not stand before a group and present her material clearly and convincingly. To a few—yes; but before a hundred—never!*

This speaker did not do her homework. She was not prepared for her speaking situation. She should have called

_____

*"When Making That Presentation," *Management Solutions*, December 1988.

someone on the municipal council ahead of time and found out how many and what groups of people would be attending her presentation. She could have then prepared herself and her presentation for a larger group.

EXAMPLE 2: PLANNING ENSURES THAT YOUR DELIVERY GOES SMOOTHLY

Assessing your speaking situation ahead of time ensures that your presentation is on target and that your delivery goes smoothly. Consider the following story.

Lisa worked for a research group in a major computer company. While at this company, Lisa had been working on a contract with the Army for a year. It was time to go back to the Army and give them a project review. The presentation to the Army was to include a live demonstration of the work completed in the past year. Lisa generally knew who would be attending the presentation, so she prepared her slides and packed up a computer to ship on the plane so that she could give a live demonstration of her work. Lisa even made a videotape of the demonstration in case something went wrong with the computer.

The plan was to give the project review in the morning, present the demonstration promptly after lunch, and then move on to future work with the army in the afternoon. As it turned out, some cables needed to be run so that the computer could be hooked up, so while the morning group was giving its presentation, people were running around trying to hook up the computer. Of course, as Murphy's Law would dictate, when they finally hooked up the computer, they found out it didn't work, so the live demonstration wasn't possible. That was OK because Lisa had brought a videotape of the live demonstration. Well, Murphy was at it again because the tape Lisa had brought was a VHS tape, and the Army had only beta machines at this particular site.

Oh well, so much for any type of demonstration of the work that the Army had funded for the past year.

The day only got worse after this point, because management had changed recently and the Army was shifting its focus—it didn't want to fund any more work in this particular area, so the whole three-year project was canceled after only one year.

Lisa came across two surprises in this presentation that could have been avoided with proper planning. First, she found out that she wasn't going to be able to show the Army her demonstration, and second, she had no idea that some of the key players in charge of the project had changed. Better planning would have helped Lisa's presentation. At a minimum, Lisa should have called ahead to find out what kind of video machines the Army had at its facility. If the Army couldn't get a VHS machine, Lisa could have arranged for one to be there. With even more research, Lisa could have found out that the Army was shifting the focus of its research, and she could have targeted her presentation on future work in the direction that the Army was taking.

Besides helping you avoid surprises in your presentation, planning your presentation gives you a mechanism for breaking the ice on preparing your presentation. Once you start answering questions about who is going to be in the audience, and at what facility you will be speaking, you start breaking down any mental blocks you have about preparing your presentation.

DEFINING YOUR PURPOSE

Clarity of thought is a prerequisite to clarity of communication. The first thing you need to do is to decide what the real purpose of your presentation is. Your presentation needs a clearly defined purpose. In particular, you need to clearly answer these questions:

- Why are you communicating information to this specific group?
- What do you hope to gain from the interaction?
- How will audience members benefit from what you have to say?
- Why wouldn't it be more beneficial to place the information in written form and distribute it?

The first step toward clarifying the purpose of your presentation is to classify the purpose of your presentation.

Classify Your Purpose

Most people, when they deliver a presentation, want to inform, persuade, or entertain their audience, or some combination of these purposes. Chances are that you can classify your purpose into one or more of these three categories. The format of your presentation will vary according to how you classify the purpose of your presentation. Let's look briefly at what your presentation needs to include if you want to inform, persuade, or entertain your audience.

Inform. Maybe you want to increase the audience's awareness about a specific topic. Presentations that inform include project status reviews and technical presentations at conferences. A presentation that informs increases the audience's level of awareness regarding the topic, or gives the audience information that it might use to perform some activity. When you inform the audience about a topic, you need to be aware of how much people in the audience already know about the topic and then move them to a new level of awareness.

Persuade.   Maybe you want your presentation to persuade the audience to think or act differently. The change you want from the audience might be a general one, such as a change of attitude regarding the role of the federal government in foreign affairs, or it might be a one-time occurrence, such as persuading a group to make a specific purchase. In either case, your presentation must not only give the audience members information that they do not already know, but it must also motivate them to use that information.

Entertain.   At a social affair, after a dinner, or at a celebration, you might want to give a less serious presentation that amuses and entertains the audience. This type of presentation requires a special style of delivery and preparation.

Using these three categories, how do you classify your presentation? Take a minute to think it over and then write down which category or categories apply to your presentation.

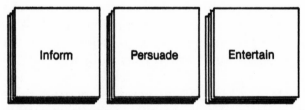

How would you classify the purpose of your presentation?

Write Your Statement of Purpose

Once you have generally classified the purpose of your presentation into the appropriate category or combination of categories, write out a single statement describing what you want to achieve from your communication. This statement of purpose will guide you through most of the decisions you will make while you prepare your speech. Use the following guidelines when you write your statement of purpose.

Make it active. Use clear verbs and describe, from the recipient's point of view, what should happen, for example, "to understand how to use the new accounting procedures," or "to purchase a six-month supply of our industrial cleaner."

Be specific. To quantify the effectiveness of your presentation, use specific language and state what will be different, for instance, "to reduce errors by at least 20 percent within next quarter," or "to identify five areas for potential cost savings."

Keep it feasible. Evaluate how much you can achieve given the amount of time available. A common rule of thumb is to allocate two to four minutes for every point you make. For example, for a five- to seven-minute speech, focus on clearly communicating two or three points.

ANALYZING YOUR AUDIENCE

Once you have written down the purpose of your presentation, consider who you will be addressing. Your presentation will vary greatly with your audience. The more you know ahead of time about your audience, the better your chances of not having any surprises. Many experienced speakers make a point to interview several of the members of the audience before their presentation.

Build a Composite Audience Member

What do most of the audience members have in common? What is the average age? Does the audience include mostly

Know your audience: Two different audiences can have
drastically different reactions to the same presentation.

men or women? Upper management, middle, or hourly?
How much schooling? Cultural background? Why will they
be at your presentation? What can you generalize about
their interests and information level on the topic? These
questions are crucial to an effective presentation. Although
you will have a variety of individuals in any group, you can
determine the best way to present your message by identi-
fying the common traits of the audience.

You might have the same message to communicate to very different groups, but the way you present the message, the points you choose to emphasize, the type and amount of supporting evidence you use, and the logic you employ will vary according to the group. An important factor in your analysis is the level of expertise the audience members have on the topic that you are presenting. You must be several levels higher than them in your familiarity with the topic to have enough credibility for them to want to listen to you.

Establish the Probable Disposition of the Group

Are you likely to have a supportive, hostile, or neutral group for your presentation? Do they feel strongly toward the topic and have a heavy investment in what you have to say, or are they learning about the topic for the first time? What is their disposition toward you? Have they seen you before so that they have a preestablished opinion of your qualifications and expertise? What will they have heard about you? Who will introduce you, and what will that person have to say? (Maybe you want to write your own introduction to start your presentation off on the right foot.) What is the reputation of the person who is introducing you, with whom you will be associated? Although it is possible to take a reading of the audience during your introduction, it will be hard to make changes to your presentation at that time. Attempt to predict the attitudes of your audience beforehand.

The last ingredient in determining the disposition of the group is to answer these questions. What do they expect? What do they think your presentation is about? If they do not know much about the topic of your presentation, you will want to spend more time outlining the purpose of your presentation. If they view your presentation as a cure-all for many of their problems, you will have to clearly define the parameters of your discussion and limit their expectations.

Estimate the Size of the Group

Knowing the size of your audience helps establish a mental image of your presentation, which is valuable to your preparation. If you have a small audience, your presentation can be more informal with a greater emphasis on discussion. With a small group you have many chances to correct and modify your statements. As the size of the audience increases, your communication will be more one-way and more formal. Presentations to larger groups need to be easy to understand. Points must be fewer and better supported, visuals must be simple and easy to comprehend, and your style must be amplified so that gestures and volume are easily understood.

ESTABLISHING THE SETTING

Before your presentation you have a significant amount of control over factors involving your speaking environment. You have this control only if you think about the presentation setting ahead of time. For instance, it does not matter how effective your presentation is if the majority of audience members are upset because they had difficulty finding parking places. Most problems with the presentation setting can be corrected in advance.

Overall Purpose of the Meeting

You have already considered the purpose of your particular presentation, but what is the purpose of the meeting itself? Is the audience being assembled to listen to you, or will you be sharing the platform with other speakers? If you are the main attraction, you need to ensure that all accommodations are perfect. Otherwise, any problems that audience members experience will reflect on the effectiveness of your presentation.

What is the tone of the occasion? Is it somber and serious, or routine and informal? Is it a one-time presentation called for to solve a specific problem, or is it a status report for a three-year-old committee meeting? The tone or atmosphere of the speaking event should be a factor in the design and delivery of your presentation.

Chronological Timing of Your Presentation

An afternoon presentation right after lunch had better be exciting and involve the audience or most of it will be lost to digestion. Likewise, meetings at the end of the day or just before lunch will have audience members watching the time. Common sense dictates that presentations given on Friday afternoons will have the same timing problems. You might also consider the schedule of activities of the organization such as paydays, holidays, and peak business times during the month. On a yearly basis, presentations might be less effective during the budget process of the company if most people are preoccupied with that activity, or during summer months, when key decision makers may be on vacation.

Length of Your Presentation

Professional presenters are conscious and considerate of time, and you should be too. Specifically seek out the time parameters allocated to you. Plan on timing your practice presentations. Have a method of tracking time while you are speaking. If you forget your watch, borrow one or have a member of the audience signal you when time is running low.

Do not go over the time limit or back down on a time commitment given to the group. Adjust your presentation if the sessions are running too long or short. If you have an occasional need to go beyond a prearranged time, ask permission of the group. Poll the group to see if they need a break.

Location of Your Presentation

Will your presentation be at or away from the office? If it is at the office, plan on a greater number of interruptions, latecomers, and early goers. It is likely that many of the audience members will be distracted by problems at the office and will not be concentrating fully on your presentation. An off-site presentation will have a more captive audience, especially if there is limited access to telephones.

Find out how the facilities meet the needs of the audience, the presentation, and yourself. You will probably need some type of audiovisual equipment that needs to be set up and tested well in advance of the presentation. If you are operating the equipment yourself, you will need to find out how to use it, and you will need to verify that it functions properly.

What type of chairs will your audience members have? Soft armchairs are desirable if they have to sit for an extended length of time. Plastic chairs or straight-backed chairs are more appropriate if you anticipate problems in holding the audience's attention. How will the room be configured? A circular or U-shaped arrangement encourages discussion between audience members. Chairs grouped together at tables encourages a team atmosphere, and chairs placed in rows, all pointing at the speaker, is a standard one-way lecture format.

Is the room carpeted? This is a very important detail for promoting a relaxed atmosphere, as well as for saving your feet if you are going to be standing for a long time. Is the lighting adequate for reading, and can it be shut off if there is a film or slide presentation? Will you have a lectern? Will you have a microphone if needed?

Your evaluation of the location and facilities gives you an accurate visual portrayal of what it will feel like to give your presentation when it comes time. If possible, you should visit the actual room you will be speaking in and plan to give at least one practice presentation in the same room. A complete list of room arrangement options are presented later in this book.

Chapter Four

Preparing Your Presentation

An effective presentation includes an introduction that catches everyone's attention, a structure that fits the information you want to present, and a conclusion that reviews the main points of your presentation. This chapter describes a formula for developing a presentation that leaves your audience where you want them to be.

PUTTING YOUR INITIAL THOUGHTS ON PAPER

You should ask two questions when determining what is to be included in your presentation:

- What can you tell the audience that they do not already know (or what information do you want them to remember from your presentation)?
- What information will convince the audience (or what would convince you if you were a member of the audience)?

The first step in preparing your presentation is to write down all the ideas that come to mind when you answer these questions. Don't be critical of any of your ideas—just let your mind wander and write them all down. You can throw out the bad ones later on. After you have all of your thoughts

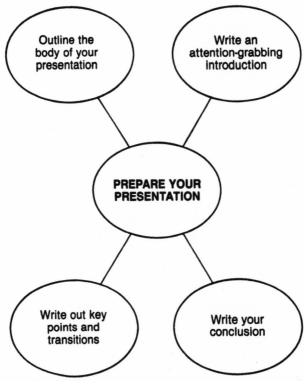

Prepare your presentation.

on paper, place them in order from most important to least important. Keep this prioritized list in mind as you prepare the body of your presentation.

PREPARING THE BODY OF YOUR PRESENTATION

It's usually easiest to outline the body of your presentation before you develop the introduction and conclusion because the body is the central part of your message; the introduction and conclusion are the trimmings. Often, you'll think of clever ideas for your introduction and conclusion while you are preparing the body.

The body of your presentation contains the key points you want to convey along with supporting data for those points. You need to pick an organization that best fits your purpose, audience, and personal delivery style.

Choosing a Format

There are numerous ways to logically present your information. You should pick a format that fits your presentation. For example, you will probably want to select a persuasive format if you want to convince or sell the audience on some concept. Alternatively, you might want to choose a chronological format to educate the audience on a particular topic. Finally, you might want to use a comparison and contrast format to elicit a decision from the audience. Following is a description of a variety of different formats for organizing your presentation.

Persuasive formats.   Many presenters want to persuade their audience to buy their product or to see things their way. Let's look at some ways to organize your presentation to persuade your audience.

1. *Proposition and proof.*   This form of organization goes back to the famous Greek orator Aristotle. With the proposition and proof format, you state your position in the beginning of your presentation, and then you dedicate the remainder of the presentation to justifying or proving your position to the audience. This format is a very straightforward method of persuasion. You logically move the audience step by step to a conclusion. It is best to use this format when everyone in the audience is familiar with your topic—that way you can spend your time proving your premise rather than explaining background information to the uninformed.

2. *Problem/solution.* The problem/solution format derives from the scientific problem-solving pattern. In this approach you first define the problem and then you explore possible solutions, citing feasible alternatives. The preferred alternative, or best solution, is saved for last. In this way less desirable alternatives are considered and rejected, leaving the speaker's proposal as the most desirable. This is an extremely effective format for persuasion, especially when the problem is complicated and the audience is either unfamiliar with the topic or hostile to your proposal. It is also effective as a teaching device because the audience is systematically carried through an indicative development of the topic and alternatives are mutually considered by speaker and audience member.

3. *Psychological progression.* This format is similar to the problem/solution format. It also follows a natural decision-making psychology, which makes it a persuasive style to employ. This format takes the audience members through a series of steps that, after arousing their interest in the introduction, seeks to dissatisfy them. As the presentation continues, you clarify the area of dissatisfaction through the information you present, and finally you illustrate concrete results and benefits that come from your proposal. The psychological progression is similar to the problem/solution format, but it focuses on the individual needs and feelings of the audience members.

Examples of persuasive formats. Following are three presentations on the same topic that employ the three different techniques of persuasion: proposition and proof, problem/solution, and psychological progression. Each of these presentations wants to convince the audience that the brand of automobile, the Toyorolla, costs the consumer less per year than any other car on the market.

1. Proposition and Proof. With this format, you state your premise up front and then you spend the rest of the presentation proving your premise. Following is an outline of the Toyorolla presentation in the proposition and proof format.

Purpose: Persuade the audience that Toyorollas are the best buy for the money.

Premise: Toyorollas give consumers the most for their money.

A. Study of different cars driven in America in the past five years.
B. The study surveyed three different factors about automobiles:
   - Average purchase price of the automobile.
   - Average life of the automobile.
   - Average maintenance cost per year of the automobile.
C. Results of the study:

Auto	Price	Life (years)	Life Maint	Cost per Year
Toyorolla	$14,000	8	$8,000	$2,750
Car A	$ 8,000	4	$4,000	$3,000
Car B	$25,000	8	$12,000	$4,625

2. Problem/solution. With the problem/solution format, you first define a problem and then explore various solutions to the problem throughout your presentation. Following is the outline for the Toyorolla presentation in the problem/solution format.

Purpose: Convince the audience that buying a Toyorolla will reduce their automobile costs.

Problem: How can you reduce your automobile costs?

A. Alternative #1: Buy an expensive car.

Main drawback: Expensive cars tend to last a long time, but maintenance tends to be more expensive.

Auto	Price	Life (years)	Life Maint	Cost per Year
Car A	$40,000	10	$20,000	$6,000
Car B	$30,000	8	$10,000	$5,000
Car C	$25,000	8	$12,000	$4,625

B. Alternative #2: Buy an inexpensive car.

Main drawback: Inexpensive cars don't last very long and thus they really aren't inexpensive.

Auto	Price	Life (years)	Life Maint	Cost per Year
Car D	$8,000	4	$4,000	$3,000
Car E	$8,000	5	$8,000	$3,200
Car F	$9,000	4	$4,000	$3,250

C. Alternative #3: Buy a medium-priced car—in particular, the Toyorolla gives you the most for your money.

Auto	Price	Life (years)	Life Maint	Cost per Year
Toyorolla	$14,000	8	$8,000	$2,750
Car G	$18,000	6	$6,000	$4,000
Car H	$19,000	7	$7,000	$3,714

3. Psychological progression. With the psychological progression format, you seek to dissatisfy the group in the first part of your presentation, and then you illustrate how you can reduce or eliminate that dissatisfaction. Here's the Toyorolla presentation using the psychological progression format.

Purpose: Convince the audience members that they are wasting money (or giving it away) when they buy other brands of cars. Show them how the Toyorolla is the best buy on the market.

A. The average person spends at least $3,000 every year on his or her automobile—that's about 10 percent of the national average income—and automobile expenses aren't even tax deductible.

B. Where's all that money going to?
   • Average maintenance cost per year is $1,000.
   • Average purchase price is $17,000.
   • Average auto life is four years.

C. Will purchasing a more inexpensive car reduce these costs?

   No. Inexpensive cars don't last very long and thus they really aren't inexpensive.

Auto	Price	Life (years)	Life Maint	Cost per Year
Car D	$8,000	4	$4,000	$3,000
Car E	$8,000	5	$8,000	$3,200
Car F	$9,000	4	$4,000	$3,250

D. Maybe purchasing an expensive car that lasts longer is the solution.

   No. Expensive cars tend to last a long time, but maintenance tends to be more expensive.

Auto	Price	Life (years)	Life Maint	Cost per Year
Car A	$40,000	10	$20,000	$6,000
Car B	$30,000	8	$10,000	$5,000
Car C	$25,000	8	$12,000	$4,625

E. How about a medium-priced car?

   Yes. There's only one medium-priced car that gives you the most for your money—the Toyorolla.

Auto	Price	Life (years)	Life Maint	Cost per Year
Toyorolla	$14,000	8	$8,000	$2,750
Car G	$18,000	6	$6,000	$4,000
Car H	$19,000	7	$7,000	$3,714

These examples illustrate that the proposition proof format is a very straightforward method of persuasion. The problem/solution format is a persuasive format that leads the audience to a logical conclusion. Psychological progression gets people's emotions involved and leads the audience to a logical and emotional conclusion.

If you do not plan on persuading your audience, there are a variety of other formats available for your presentation. Following is a summary of some of the other types of formats you can use.

Chronological format. A chronological organization relates a process or series of events that are presented in the order in which they occurred. Chronological formats are well suited to presentations that take a historical view of a problem or situation or have a narrative tone throughout.

Cause and effect format. This format first outlines various causes and then describes the effects of each. It is useful for examining possible future events. For example, if event A leads to B and B leads to C, what are the chances that event C will occur, and if it does, what can we do about it? This organization can be reversed so that effects or results are first discussed and then possible causes are considered. This reverse format is useful for analyzing a present problem.

Comparison and contrast format. This format examines how several things are similar and how they are different, which is often a valuable process for deciding between alternative actions.

Order of decreasing importance format. This method lists information from most important to least important, and can be especially effective in making sure an important piece of information is not missed by the audience. Attention is usually greatest toward the beginning of a presentation. The reverse of this format—increasing order of importance—is effective in adding a dramatic or suspenseful flair to your presentation.

Simple to complex format. This organization starts with simpler concepts and builds to more complex and abstract ones. It is effective for teaching because you begin with what the audience currently knows and gradually introduce more advanced ideas. The reverse organization, sometimes called backward chaining, explains the big picture to the audience and then the specific subelements that make up that complicated process. For example, in explaining how a computer works, you must first describe the general theory of how a computer works before you relate a step-by-step description of what happens.

Classification format. This method organizes information in convenient categories for presenting and remembering that information. It is an effective method for breaking up a list of items so that the presentation does not become boring or difficult to follow, as is often the case when a speaker announces that he or she will present 14 reasons for accepting a proposal.

Physical location format. This is an effective format for certain types of presentations, such as a descriptive presentation of a new office complex. This method follows a visual pattern for what is being discussed, such as the exterior of the building, the interior, adjacent facilities, and convenience of parking locations. The format can also be used in describing geographical information.

Experiment with Different Formats

Use the following list of formats and check off which best fit your purpose, audience, and style of delivery.

Proposition and proof	_____
Problem / solution	_____
Psychological progression	_____
Chronological	_____
Cause and effect	_____
Comparison and contrast	_____
Order of decreasing importance	_____
Simple to complex	_____
Classification	_____
Physical location	_____

Try writing out your main points using or combining the formats you checked off. Experiment with different formats to discover which are most effective for your purpose, audience, and style of delivery.

Select Supporting Data

Once you have written out the main points of your presentation in a selected format, you need to back up your main points with supporting data. Supporting data serve several purposes in your presentation. Most importantly, they add credibility to your statements. When data are used appropriately, statements and opinions take on a factual tone that makes your presentation more convincing.

Supporting information can also be used to clarify a point you are trying to make. When a point is complex or abstract, additional information or data can help an audience to visualize and more easily comprehend your meaning. Because different people learn best in various ways, examples, data, or other supporting information will increase the

Supporting data add credibility to your presentation.

percentage of audience members who comprehend and are convinced by your arguments. A third reason for using supporting information in a presentation is to make it more interesting. Examples and stories break up the presentation of information and focus the group's attention. Audience members typically enjoy stories and often will remember them long after other points in your presentation are forgotten.

Following is a discussion of the most common types of supporting data that you can incorporate in your presentation.

Statistics. Statistics are numbers, percentages, dollars, and facts. They can add instant credibility to a statement and make your opinion sound like a fact. Most listeners will believe a statement that begins, "A recent study indicated that . . ." Statistics can be manipulated to your advantage in your presentation. For example, if your company sold 400,000 units of a certain product, which represented a 3 percent increase in units sold, you would use the 400,000 units if you wanted to create the impression that the sales were significant and the 3 percent if you wanted to make the same sales seem insignificant. Statistics are most effective when you give the audience a comparison they can easily relate to. For example, a new type of paint may cover 600 square feet per can, which is not necessarily impressive unless you know that a typical can of paint covers only 350 square feet. The closer the comparison is to the listeners' experience and the more surprising the contrast is to the listener, the more impressive and convincing the information will be. Another way of making statistics stand out more is to round off numbers. For example, 5,779 can become "almost 6,000," 332 can become "hundreds," and March through June can become "a quarter of a year."

Examples. Examples are representative cases of an occurrence or an object. Use examples to clarify a confusing statement or to bring a vague, general abstraction down to a specific application. One risk in using examples is that the example you use might be discredited by the audience as being an isolated case. To make your examples more credible, try to indicate why it is a typical and representative example. To support the contention that "quality assurance in manufacturing is difficult to maintain," do not simply state, "I went down to observe the production line twice this week and both times rejection rates were high," but rather, "Two randomly selected days in which production was normal showed high rejection rates, which correlated with industrywide feelings concerning quality assurance." Another way of making examples more effective is to use examples from your personal experience. This will keep them from sounding academic or contrived and will enhance the credibility you have in the topic.

Stories. Stories are expanded examples, which serve to reinforce a specific point. They are almost always welcomed by members of the audience because people usually enjoy listening to stories. As with examples, the accounting of an event or occurrence can make a point clearer because it is easier to "see" a graphic description than to envision words and concepts. The disadvantage of stories is that they are difficult to use effectively. Speakers often make the mistake of being too long-winded and giving unnecessary details, rambling, or going off track onto an unrelated tangent. At other times, speakers become redundant and backtrack so that the story becomes boring and the audience becomes anxious for the speaker to get to the point. Stories are most effective when there is a logical order and movement to what you say. Make sure that the story ties in well with the information presented both before and after the story itself. Work on your style by practicing in your everyday conversations the dramatic or suspenseful relaying of experiences. The ability to weave an interesting yarn will always be an asset.

Quotations. Quotations add a certain class and formality to your presentations, but, like examples, they do not prove your points. One disadvantage is that it is usually relatively easy to find an opposing quote for any quotation. For that reason quotations should not be relied upon as evidence for your presentation, but rather as support for the style and delivery of your communication. The value of a quote inevitably rests upon how well known the originator is. Sometimes it is best to directly read a quote for the added emphasis it will bring to your presentation. You may use the indicators "quote" and "end quote" when being formal, otherwise it will suffice to simply lead off with the quote by saying: "One expert states that . . ." or "In the words of . . ."

Write Your Transitions

A smooth presentation requires smooth transitions between the main points in your presentation. Transitions start with the current thought and explain a reason or rationale for moving to the next thought. Good transitions keep your audience right with you. Planning out your transitions ahead of time helps your presentation in the following ways.

Emphasize your organization. Transitions are your opportunity to emphasize what you've covered already and where you are headed. This will help the audience understand where they've been and where they are going. If you were giving a presentation that used a chronological format, you might say something like, "So in the last five years our company has been devoted to researching a system that would best meet your needs. Now we have developed the system and this is our plan for the next five years."

Grab the audience's attention. You may have lost the audience during the last point you made. You can throw an attention getter in your transition to wake the audience up and get them ready for your next point.

Help you remember the flow of your presentation. Having your transitions planned out links the main points of your presentation together and helps you remember what you need to say when you deliver your presentation.

WRITING YOUR INTRODUCTION

A good introduction grabs your audience's attention and prepares it for what you have to say. It states the premise of the presentation and indicates why the topic is significant to audience members. It creates desire in the audience to know more about what you have to say. Your introduction paves the way for the rest of your presentation.

A good introduction must grab the audience's attention.

The importance of a well-planned, effective introduction cannot be stressed enough. Although it is not a fair practice, most audience members judge you and your presentation based on only the first few minutes of contact. Unfortunately, you do not get a second chance to make your first impression. Even the shortest presentations need a well-planned opening. Without an interested and alert audience, your presentation doesn't stand a chance of being effective. You need to involve the audience in your presentation by mentally pulling them into the topic, or, at times, even physically involving them, as in a show of hands or solicitations of an overt response. An effective introduction captures the audience's attention in a relevant way, places them and yourself at ease, previews what you have to say, and explains the significance of your message. Let's examine why and how we can best fulfill these four purposes and then detail a variety of effective introductions that you might use.

Capture the Audience's Attention

Most audiences are not mentally with a speaker when he or she first begins to speak. They are in their own worlds, planning what they will be doing later that day, thinking about a problem they are having, or just plain daydreaming. Initially, audience members observe rather that listen to a speaker. They will notice your manner, dress, and other nonverbal aspects and use those to form an opinion about your credibility. An effective introduction pulls the wandering minds into the room and specifically focuses the attention of the audience on you and your topic. A few moments of preparation for an effective opening will keep you from charging off and leaving your audience behind. If members of an audience tune in to what you are saying in the middle of a sentence several minutes after you have begun to speak, you can be sure that they will be confused and miss the point of many of the items you are relating. Their attention will revert to the previous mental activity they were engaged in. An attention getter increases the chances that your audience will be with you as you proceed to the body of your message.

Any effective attention getter must be relevant to the topic of discussion or the immediate speaking situation. There are numerous inappropriate ways to grab the attention of a group. For example, many speakers automatically begin presentations with the latest joke they have heard whether it is relevant to the situation or not. Don't make this mistake. If you cannot tie your attention getter in with your topic, choose another opening. Let's consider how one speaker took a play on words and made it into an effective, appropriate opening: "I called the driving school this morning and they signed me up for a crash course. In the next ten minutes I want to drive home the point that automobile safety is no accident."

Following are some of the most common methods for opening a presentation and getting the attention of the audience.

Ask a question.   Ask either a rhetorical question or one that seeks an overresponse from the audience. Either type will involve the audience by getting it to think about the topic. If you want the audience members to respond, make sure it is easy for them to do so. Ask a question that can be answered with a yes or a no, or call for a show of hands. Here are some examples:

- How many in this room have ever been confused about federal tax forms?
- Would you know what to do if the person next to you started choking?
- Who here owns an imported car?

Starting out with a question in your introduction also helps you learn information about the audience, which can then be used to tailor the remainder of your presentation.

State an impressive fact.   Begin with an unusual and impressive fact or statistic that supports the theme of your presentation. Examples include the following:

- The number of our competitors has doubled in the last five years.

- One person out of every five in this room will die of cancer.
- More people will watch TV tonight than the total number of people that have seen all the stage performances of all Shakespeare's plays.

Tell a joke.   This is a traditional way for a speaker to warm up to an audience. Be sure the joke is appropriate. If you have any doubts, select another joke or a different method of beginning. Also be sure that the joke can be made to be relevant to the topic being discussed or the speaking situation. Some people are better at using one-liners, and others can be effective with a longer humorous story. Experiment with each and see what works best for you. You might be safer to start with a joke that you particularly liked while you were in another audience. Keep track of such jokes in a small booklet, and soon you will have an entire library to adapt to various situations.

Tell a story.   A personal story that relates an experience you had with some aspect of the topic being discussed is an excellent way to begin a presentation. People are drawn to hearing about the experiences of others, and in the presentational setting such a story also enhances your credibility. Stories are easy to visualize and are thus effective for communicating information.

Use a quotation.   Quotations make for interesting introductions for presentations. You can always find a quote that fits the topic and perhaps even the situation. Quotations add to the credibility of your presentation and your style of delivery.

Make an emphatic statement.   A forceful statement captures the attention of your audience as well as sets a dynamic tone for the remainder of your presentation. An example is, "It's time we stop letting the high cost of quality tools eat up our profits!"

No matter which type of introduction you select, make it upbeat, positive, and surefire. It is the part of your presentation that is probably worth practicing a few times more than other parts of your speech. Following are some other suggestions to consider concerning your introduction.

Put the Audience and Yourself at Ease

You want to give your audience a chance—no matter how brief—to get to know you before you can expect them to trust the information you have to communicate. An effective introduction relaxes both the audience and yourself. One reason why humor is so popular in an introduction is that laughter gives everyone an energy release, which instantly improves the attitude of the listeners. This is often referred to as warming up the audience. It sets a mutually acceptable tone for your presentation. A speaker who continues delivering information when he or she senses that the audience is not in tune with the presentation is asking for trouble throughout the remainder of the delivery.

Preview the Topic

To eliminate the possibility of any confusion, the speaker should clearly state the purpose of the presentation. The purpose, which you determined in your preliminary analysis, should be stated in terms of what the audience can expect from the forthcoming presentation. For example, you may want to begin this part of your introduction with words such as, "Before leaving today, each person present should have a better understanding of . . ." or, "After hearing this presentation the audience will be able to . . ."

State the Significance of the Topic

Very few topics are automatically perceived as relevant to all members of your audience. Even if the benefits of your presentation seem obvious to you, it is a good habit to take a moment to explain why your presentation is of value to everyone in the audience. Chances are that even those who initially believed your presentation would be of value probably focused on only a single benefit. You can provide several reasons for which your presentation will be beneficial. Your significance statement should be worded from the listener's perspective so that it touches a personal level for members of the audience. Say, "This presentation will show you how to save hundreds of dollars on your next car purchase," instead of, "This presentation will discuss possible savings when purchasing a car." You want to suggest that the information to be presented will have a real, immediate value for the listener—that the communication is not an academic exercise but has very practical applications.

Not only should you explain why the topic is important to the audience, but you should also indicate why the topic is especially timely. What makes your information more important today than it was last year or will be next year? What are the possible consequences if action is not taken soon? These are questions you should consider in building a sense of urgency and a freshness for the topic. Your statement of significance is an excellent way to conclude your introduction because it creates an interest. It provides a reason for the audience members to want to continue to give their attention to you. Some speakers effectively emphasize the significance of the presentation by concluding the introduction with a question such as, "Is 10 minutes of your undivided attention worth the benefits I just described? If so, listen closely."

Don't Be Negative

Do not apologize for lack of preparation or any other inadequacy you might feel about your speaking situation. Do not insult or offend your audience. Instead focus on what is positive about the situation, the group, and what you have to offer. Be confident in your manner and your word selection. Be enthusiastic about speaking and avoid mundane starts such as, "Today I'm going to talk about. . ." or, "Mr. So and So asked me to give this talk."

Be Concise and Dynamic

An introduction should be brief. It should start strong and pull the audience into the topic of the presentation. Do not ramble or in other ways be long-winded in your opening remarks. Don't buffer your first statement with comments such as, "Before I begin my presentation, I would like to take a few minutes to . . ." or, "I guess the best way to start is to give you a description of all my previous experience with this type of problem." Either of these is guaranteed to put your audience to sleep, perhaps before you finish the sentence.

WRITING YOUR CONCLUSION

A conclusion reviews what you have discussed in your presentation in a way that makes the key points of your message memorable to the audience. Most conclusions have some type of call to action in which the speaker suggests that audience members do or think something different as a result of the information that was just presented. Most of what has been said for the introduction applies to the conclusion as well. Your closing should be planned in an exacting way. It should be brief and motivational. Following are some tips for writing your conclusion.

Review Your Main Points

Summarize the points you made, focusing not so much on what was said as what should be remembered and why those items are significant. Repeat the purpose of the speech and the main points that you defended throughout, or rephrase this information.

Give a Call to Action

Most presentations intend to change the thinking or behavior of the audience, so make clear to each member of the group exactly what he or she should do if convinced by your presentation.

Tie Back to the Introduction

Your presentation appears polished and well planned if you return to your introductory remarks. Add on to a story you used to start your presentation, making a new twist, insight, or explanation.

Don't Ramble On

Do not continue talking after you have finished your prepared presentation. Don't say, "Another thing I want to mention," or "One more item I wanted to cover is . . ." If you are ever at a loss for words as you approach the close, simply repeat your contention and sit down. No new information should ever be presented in your conclusion, especially not if it was something that you simply forgot to mention. No one will be the wiser that you failed to include the information.

Don't Just Stop

You need a smooth closing to your presentation, not an abrupt ending that leaves the audience members scratching their heads. Never say, "And that's all I have to say," or any other type of apology such as, "I'm sorry I wasn't better prepared, but I hope you picked up something."

PREPARING NOTES FOR YOUR PRESENTATION

Notes help you remember exactly what you want to communicate and give you a greater sense of confidence in your delivery. You can always refer to your notes during your presentation if you forget what your next point is. Following are some pointers for preparing notes for your presentation. At the end of this chapter you will find some sample notes for an hour-long presentation on job hunting, given to about 50 people.

Use an Outline Format

Your notes should be divided into major and minor headings, arranged in the categories just discussed: the introduction, body, and conclusion. Use space, capitalization, or underlining to highlight your key points, and indent supporting information.

Be Brief but Specific

Write just enough on your notes to remember the entire thought you wish to convey. Usually this can be key words or statistics you want to be sure to communicate accurately. Do not simply say "story" because you may forget exactly what story you had in mind. Instead state something unique about the story that will more likely jar your memory, such as "Jones account story," to convey an example you have from a recent interaction with a customer of yours. When you practice with your notes, you will find that each time you present your material, your outline will have shorter reminders for each point.

Write Large Enough to Read

Your notes will not do you much good if you cannot easily read them during your delivery. Print boldly so that this will not be a problem.

Write Out the Key Parts

Because the exact wording is crucial for certain parts of your presentation, write those parts out: a single sentence for each major point, the exact word you will begin and end your presentation with, and transitional sentences between major sections of your speech. The transitions are written out because of the tendency to inadvertently omit them during delivery.

Make Notes to Yourself

Indicate, for example, where you plan to use a visual aid. If you are using several visual aids, number them for easy reference. Also make notes in the margin to help you check delivery mistakes you tend to make, such as, "STEADY EYE CONTACT," "PAUSE FOR EMPHASIS," or "SLOW DOWN."

Sample Notes for a Presentation

Following are some sample notes for an hour-long presentation of job hunting, given to a group of about 50 people.

SAMPLE PRESENTATION NOTES

The Truth behind Job Hunting

INTRODUCTION

Attention

"How many people here know how to hitchhike?" (hitchhiking analogy)

Transition

"Job hunting is a lot like hitchhiking."

Significance

8 mil unemployed in the U.S.

Avg. American chgs. job every 3.6 years (twice as fast as 10 years ago).

Chances are in 1–2 years you will be in the job market.

Transition

Will you know what to do? Most people don't.

BODY

Problem

Typical approach

(1) *Secondary sources* (want ads, personal, agencies)

(2) *Impersonal* (form letters not to a specific person)

(3) *Limited leads* 3–5 (disadvantages: waiting/wasting time/rejection felt personally/feeling of starting over/treadmill attitude/behavior slump)

Transition

"It doesn't have to be that way. There is an alternative."

Solution

Alternative approach: 3 P's

      (1) **Primary** sources (those who you would work directly for)

      (2) **Personal** contacts (phone, individual letters, follow-up)

      (3) **Plenty** of leads (advantages: expanding network of contacts active and confident, rejection less personal [too busy to care], better chance of offers)

Transition

    "That's the way it works, and it can work for you!"

CONCLUSION

Review

    "The three P's—Primary sources, approached in a Personal way, and Plenty of them!"

Action and Twist to Tie Intro

    "Use these techniques and you will never need to 'hitchhike' for a job again!"

Questions:

PRESENTATION WORKSHEET

INTRODUCTION
Attention-getting statement:

_____

_____

_____

Purpose statement:

_____

_____

_____

Significance statement:

_____

_____

_____

Overview of main points:

1. _____

2. _____

3. _____

SPEECH BODY:
Main point #1:

_____

_____

_____

Supporting evidence:

_____

_____

_____

Transition:

_____

_____

_____

Main point #2:

_____

_____

_____

Supporting evidence:

_____

_____

_____

Transition:

_____

_____

_____

Main point #3:

_____

_____

Supporting evidence:

_____

_____

Transition:

_____

_____

_____

CONCLUSION
Review of main points:

1. _____

_____

_____

2. _____

_____

_____

3. _____

_____

_____

Call to action: _____

_____

_____

Chapter Five

Selecting and Preparing Visual Aids

Visual aids dominate modern presentations. They can turn a good delivery into a great one. Visual aids add emphasis and clarity to specific points of your presentation. They also emphasize the organization of your presentation and help hold the interest of the audience. Visual aids present information through another channel of communication, the visual channel, and increase the probability that your message will be effectively delivered. Let's examine the advantages and disadvantages of some of the most popular visual aids.

CHOOSING YOUR VISUAL AIDS

The most common types of visual aids are transparencies, flip charts, and 35mm slides. Often your selection depends on how much preparation time you have, how much money you can spend, what facilities are available at the location of your presentation, and what standards your organization has concerning visual aids.

Transparencies

Transparencies are the most versatile of visual aids. Transparencies are clear sheets of plastic film that can include images, graphics, and text. Transparencies can be used with groups of any size. If you have the time and the budget, professionally made transparencies are the best. Such transparencies can include nice color graphics, different colored transparencies, and overlapping sections to accent your presentation.

Advantages of transparencies.   Along with the obvious advantages associated with having visual aids to support your presentation, transparencies offer some unique advantages.

1. *Transparencies can be generated quickly.* With the advent of computer graphics, transparencies can be generated very quickly. If you have a graphics software package on a computer, you can design your presentation on your computer, print out your presentation using a graphics printer, and create the transparencies from the graphics printouts on a copier machine.

2. *Transparencies give you the flexibility of a chalkboard.* Another nice feature of transparencies on an overhead projector is that you can use the overhead projector like a chalkboard. You can write on a transparency as you speak to the audience to illustrate different points.

3. *Using transparencies helps maintain control over the audience.* Using an overhead projector has an advantage because you can have the room partially lit, and you can still face the audience while you give your presentation. Both of these factors allow you to have greater control of the audience's attention during your presentation.

4. *You can use the frame on the transparency for notes.* You can make notes on the transparency frame to help you remember points to be discussed during the presentation of that transparency.

Do's and don'ts of transparencies. Because it is so easy to create transparencies yourself, make sure you use the following guidelines.

1. *Frame your transparencies.* Transparencies have a tendency to stick together, and if you don't frame your transparencies, you will find yourself fumbling with them when you give your presentation. Put them in cardboard frames, or slip them into plastic covers, which are available in office supply stores. The plastic covers are nice because they are usually three-hole punched, which means that you can assemble your presentation in a three-ring notebook.

2. *Make sure that the information is readable on the screen.* Almost any type of information can be conveyed with transparencies, including drawings, notes, photos, letters, and so forth, but make sure that the information is readable when it is projected on a screen. Transparencies are so easy to make that you might be tempted to copy some existing chart or typed text onto a transparency! Typed information, even if is in all uppercase letters, is very difficult to read and should be avoided. Use larger sized fonts for your transparencies. Computer printouts, maps, and complicated graphs should also be avoided because of the difficulty in reading and understanding such information.

3. *Use one transparency to convey about two minutes' worth of information.* The average amount of time you spend discussing information on a transparency should be about two minutes. Don't try to cram too much information onto a single transparency.

4. *Make sure your transparencies are not boring.* Too many transparencies without enough graphics often makes for a boring presentation, especially if the audience has to read a significant amount of

information from the transparencies. Simple transparencies can be made more effective by adding arrows, dots, and other artist's trimmings. Colored sheets of transparency film can be taped over your printed message to make it visually more pleasing.

5. *Don't pile 60 transparencies in front of the audience.* If you put all of your transparencies in front of the audience members, they will wonder when you will get through them rather than paying attention. Keep your transparencies out of sight.

Don't pile your transparencies in front of the audience.

6. *Don't read from your transparencies.* It's OK to use your transparencies as a reminder of what you wanted to say—but don't read from them to the audience.

```
┌─────────────────────────────────────────┐
│  🖉  IV 1989 Budget        💵           │
├─────────────────────────────────────────┤
│                                         │
│  1. G & A                    $500,000   │
│                                         │
│  2. Capital Equipment      $1,000,000   │
│                                         │
│  3. Marketing                $500,000   │
│                                         │
└─────────────────────────────────────────┘
```

A good transparency design has (1) nice graphics, (2) large type, (3) simplified information, and (4) numbered points.

7. *Make copies of your transparencies for the audience.* It is a good idea to give your audience a copy of your transparencies in case some members of the audience can't see the screen very well, or in case audience members want to make notes on them as you go along.

Flip Charts

Also known as a chart pack, a flip chart consists of a pad of paper on an easel. Flip charts are commonly used at meetings or presentations to keep track of ideas or comments generated at a meeting.

Advantages of flip charts. You do not have to worry that something mechanical will go wrong with a flip chart—about the worst that can happen is that you'll run out of paper or your felt pens will go dry, each of which are easy problems to solve. Flip charts offer the following unique advantages:

1. *They are great for training and for making spontaneous notes.* The flip chart is excellent for making notes spontaneously while presenting to a group of 5 to

50. The flip chart is great when you are training or consulting with a group, or when you are running a business meeting. Flip charts are best suited for presentations during which you are gathering information and developing ideas.

2. *They can be prepared in advance.* Flip charts can be prepared in advance and flipped as needed during your presentation. This technique allows for more carefully drawn visuals and a chance to redo mistakes. If you prepare your flip charts in advance, you can pencil in notes to yourself that are not noticeable to the audience.

Do's and don'ts of flip charts. Here are some things to keep in mind when you are creating your flip charts.

1. *Keep your writing legible.* Take the time to write legibly. Try to keep your letters the same height. Make sure you use lined paper—this will help you letter neatly.

2. *Use colors for emphasis.* Colored markers help emphasize your points and keep your charts more interesting.

3. *Use graphics for emphasis.* You don't need to be a great artist; just use simple graphics such as lines, circles, and squares. Graphics add variety to your flip charts.

4. *Keep your points brief.* Like any visual aid, don't overload the flip chart with too much information.

35mm Slides

Slide shows can give a presentation the ultimate professional look. Making slides is relatively inexpensive, but skillfully designing and producing an effective show can be more expensive. Slide presentations are typically reserved for large formal meetings of several hundred people or more.

Advantages of 35mm slides. The overriding advantage of 35mm slides is that your presentation appears very professional. For a formal presentation, you might have to spend extra time and money preparing the slides, but it will be worth it.

Do's and don'ts of 35mm slides.

1. *You have to work extra hard to keep the audience awake.* Remember, the lights will be out when you deliver a 35mm slide presentation, and the audience members won't be watching you; they will be watching the slides. You have to make sure that your presentation is interesting enough to keep the audience awake. Incorporate lots of attention grabbers.

2. *Use color and graphics.* You've gone to the trouble to create 35mm slides for your presentation, so make sure that they are colorful and graphics filled—it'll help keep the audience with you.

3. *Use one slide to convey two minutes' worth of information.* The average length you spend discussing the information on a slide should be about two minutes. Again, be careful to limit the amount of information on a single slide.

4. *Make and illustrate your points very clearly.* You lose some of your flexibility when you give a 35mm slide presentation—you can't go make a point on a blackboard very easily—so make sure your presentation doesn't have any holes in it.

USING VISUAL AIDS

Even the best visuals can destroy a presentation if they are improperly used. The most important thing to remember is that your visual aids should *support* your presentation; they should not *be* your presentation. Avoid being the speaker who brings in a stack of overhead slides and then proceeds to speak only from those slides, hardly noticing the audience. Instead, you should always be the center of attention in your presentation. Always practice with your aid first. A diagram or a phrase that appears to make sense when you glance at it may be very difficult to explain while standing in front of a group if you have not done so before. Following are some additional tips to observe.

Have Everything in Place

Have your visual aids ready to go before the presentation. For transparencies, this may mean having the first one on the overhead, properly centered and focused, with the rest in a neat stack nearby. If you are using flip charts or other prepared visuals, post them in an appropriate position in the front of the room and cover them until it is time for your presentation. Remove all aids from previous presentations before you begin.

Don't Show Them until You're Ready

As soon as a visual is exposed, it will attract the attention of the audience. If you are still introducing the topic or the visual, chances are great that your spoken word or the visual will be missed. When using an overhead projector, you can easily control attention by turning the light on and off. On individual transparencies you can cover specific points on a list by sliding a sheet of paper between the slide and the machine, and then expose your points as you are ready.

Avoid Holding Up Visual Aids

Although this may be effective when you first show your visual, chances are that you will move while speaking, and

the visual will become distracting. Either post the visual or
have someone else hold it while you are speaking.

Speak to the Audience, Not to the Visual

Always face the audience while speaking. For effective
speaking while using a visual, *point* to the specific area of
the visual to which you are referring, *turn* to the audience,
and *speak*. Although this may add several moments to
your presentation, it will make your points more clearly
understood.

Speak to the audience, not to the visual aid.

Speak Louder when Using Visual Aids

Because your attention is distracted and the room is darker,
and because some overhead and slide projectors are noisy,
you should increase your vocal level while using visual aids.

Don't Block the View

Be careful that you, your podium, and other objects are not in the line of sight of any audience member. Be especially careful of the views from the front sides of the audience. This may take some coordination if you are using several overhead or slide projectors, so be sure to allow extra time before your presentation to arrange the room.

Use a Pointer

A pointer or a pen makes your presentation more professional and makes it easier to understand what part of the slide you are referring to. For overhead projectors, a pen or arrow may be left stationary on the machine for greater stability. A pointer helps you get out of the way of your visual.

Remove Your Visual Aids when Finished

Both after your point is complete, and when your presentation is done, remove your visuals from the sight of the audience. This again will help you to control the attention of the audience and is a presentational courtesy upon completion of your talk. However, do not pack your visual up before finishing your presentation. This is distracting for audience members and indicates that what you are saying, as you mechanically clean up, is less important.

USING HANDOUTS

Handouts with an informational presentation can be an effective means of increasing the learning and retention level of your audience. Give careful thought to the preparation and use of handouts for a presentation, or they might end up disrupting your presentation. We have several guidelines to follow when using handouts.

Decide Whether You Want the Audience Taking Notes

If handouts are distributed before or during your presentation, audience members will promptly read the material and will take notes as they listen to you speak. This can be appropriate if the purpose of your presentation is to inform. This can be distracting if the purpose of your presentation is to persuade. For persuasive presentations, it is usually a good idea to tell the audience ahead of time that you will be handing out materials at the end of the presentation, and to request that they not take notes during the presentation. For example, you might say, "I see several people taking notes—all of this is summarized in the materials you will receive, so you might prefer to simply listen for now." The material is likely be used later by audience members if you briefly summarize what is contained in the handouts when you distribute them.

Make All Handouts Self-Explanatory

Do not assume that the audience will remember the details of your presentation. Have headings, interpretive remarks, keys, and any other necessary information for the audience to fully understand the material at a later date.

Make Sure They Contribute to Your Objective

Too often speakers present handout material that is designed for some other purpose. This often makes your presentation less professional and seemingly thrown together. Like the visual aids, each handout should be essential to clear communication.

Do Not Read from Your Handouts

Your audience does not want to listen to you reading from your handouts. Most people want an interactive presentation, meaning that you look at them and not at your handouts. Reading from your handouts will cause you to lose the audience's interest and will leave them thinking that you wasted their time, as they could have read your handouts on their own.

With a minimum amount of preparation and skill in using them, visual aids and handouts can enhance your effectiveness. Many companies have graphics departments to help with designing and preparation. Use this professional resource, if it is available, because it can help broaden the number and type of ideas you might have for supporting your message.

VISUAL AIDS CHECKLIST

Following are guidelines for designing your visual aids. For each visual aid, ask yourself the following questions:

Is it essential? _____

Is it simple? _____

Is it large? _____

Is it labeled? _____

Is it interesting? _____

Are the key points numbered? _____

Use the following guidelines when you practice your presentation with your visual aids. After you have gone through your practice session, ask yourself these questions (or have a friend in the audience answer them for you):

Did I have everything in place at the start of the presentation? _____

Did I show any visual aid before I was ready? _____

Did I hold up any visual aids? _____

Did I speak to the audience, and not to the visual aid?

_____

Did I speak loud enough? _____

Did I block the view of the audience? _____

Did I use a pointer? _____

Did I remove a visual aid when I was finished? _____

Chapter Six

Practice Makes Perfect

Plan on practicing your presentation a minimum of five or six times. The more you practice, the more familiar you'll become with your outline and the better you will get. When you practice your presentation, make sure you concentrate on recalling your ideas and their flow—do not spend time practicing the specific wording of your presentation. That is, do not memorize your presentation. Nobody wants to listen to a presentation that has been memorized. Presentations that have been memorized are stiff and boring and lack spontaneity. This chapter presents some guidelines and a step-by-step method for practicing your presentation.

GUIDELINES FOR PRACTICING

There are a variety of ways you can practice your presentation. Practices can range from going over your outline in your head to practicing your presentation in front of a group in the room where your presentation will be conducted. For the most effective results, one of your practices should use the same room setup and the same visual aids you plan on using during your final delivery. Let's look at some guidelines to follow when practicing your presentation.

Make Each Practice One Step Closer to the Real Presentation

Make each practice session a little more like the real presentation. Plan out your practices. First look at how much time you have to practice your presentation. Use the planning worksheet at the end of this chapter to help develop a schedule for your practices. Map out different practice sessions for your presentation. For example, if you have time for three practice sessions, your first practice might simply be thinking through your presentation in your head. Your next practice session might involve having someone videotape you while you deliver your presentation. Finally, your third practice session might be in front of a group of your friends in the same room where you will be delivering your presentation.

Moving a step closer to the real thing gives you a sense of movement toward your final goal and keeps you from feeling like you are just rehearsing the same circumstances over and over again. The closer you make your practices to the real presentation, the less inhibited you will be on the day of your presentation. When you finally present your material, it will seem as if you have already given the presentation several times.

Finish Each Practice Presentation

Don't fall into the trap of starting your practice over from the beginning each time you stumble on your words. If you do this, during the delivery of your presentation some parts of it will be very familiar to you—and others will be unfamiliar. It is likely that you will have a strong, well-rehearsed introduction and a weak closing. Your closing is just as important as your introduction, so give them equal attention.

Continue to the end of your presentation, even if you fumble, Make a check mark on your outline to indicate where your rough spots are. When you have finished your practice session, go back to the areas that you checked off and rehearse them until you are comfortable with what you want to say. When you've smoothed over the rough spots, run through the entire presentation one more time. This technique results in a more even presentation.

Time Your Practice Presentations

After the first one or two practice deliveries, time the next few. This makes you more sensitive to your time limits and your pace of delivery. Try to speak at the same rate as you will when actually giving the presentation. Most people tend to speak faster during the real delivery than during their practice presentations. Make notes of how your practice presentations compare to your real presentation in length so that you can adjust accordingly for your next presentation.

Pay Attention to Details and Get Feedback

Perfect practice makes perfect delivery. As you become more familiar with your material and more confident with your delivery, look for ways to improve. Ask anyone who listens to your practice deliveries to recommend improvements. Use the evaluation form at the end of this chapter and have someone give you feedback on your presentation. Let's now look at a three-step method for practicing your presentation.

STEP 1: WARMING UP

Imagine that practicing your presentation is really like writing a book. Completing a practice session is like completing another draft of your book. Your first practice drafts should

Time your practice presentation.

focus on getting through the material comfortably in a steady flow. In your final drafts, you should practice your finesse. Here are three progressive steps you can take to make your initial practice sessions as easy as possible.

Prepare Your Mental Draft

There are two different ways to prepare the mental draft of your presentation: either run through your presentation in your head, or write it down on paper. You can choose either method, or perhaps you want to try both. To run through your presentation in your head, get in a comfortable position, close your eyes, and think through your presentation. Imagine the actual words you would use as you give your delivery. Refer to your notes as often as you need to. Start concentrating on your transitions—how one idea connects to another.

For some people, a smooth flow of information comes more readily when they write down what they want to say. This does not mean you should memorize your presentation. Remember, you want to have a variety of methods of in your hip pocket for describing various points in your presentation. Writing down what you want to say should be only one way of wording your information for the first practice. Each time you practice, you will improve the way your information is presented, and you will increase the number of ways that your ideas and message can be described.

Prepare Your Speaking Draft

After you have mentally gone through your presentation, try going over the presentation verbally. Strive for a nonthreatening practice: remain seated and just talk out loud as you go down your outline. Remember to keep what you are saying in the first person; for example, say, "It's an important problem we have to discuss today, one that affects each and every one of us," rather than talking to yourself and saying. "Then I'll tell them about how important the problem is." Your goal is to use the actual words, or a variety thereof, that will be used in your real presentation.

Prepare Your Standing Draft

After a few times through your talking draft, attempt the same practice technique while standing up. Make a mock podium, if you will eventually have one, for your final presentation, and begin to fill in the behavior portion of your message, that is, your gestures, eye contact, and other types on nonverbal behavior. In the same way that you are not memorizing words, do not memorize gestures. Specifically practiced gestures almost always come across as staged and artificial. Instead, try a variety of gestures that are natural to you. It is more important for you to become comfortable with your physical space around you and your ability to gesture in general, rather than trying to mimic any specific gesture. Do this by overgesturing. Wave your arms, point, stretch, pound your fist, grip your hands. Experiment to see what you find is effective for your style. At first they might all seem contrived, but with practice and less inhibition, natural gesturing will spring forth from your style.

STEP 2: GETTING FEEDBACK

After you have warmed up with thinking and speaking through your outline a number of times, you should try one or more types of practice drafts to obtain feedback for improvement. We present a few to choose from. You might even try all three for maximum insight into possible improvements.

Mirrored Draft

One of the easiest ways to get additional information about your delivery style is by practicing in front of a mirror. For many speakers, this is a simple and effective method of seeing how you come across to an audience. Other speakers find such a practice embarrassing. Try it for yourself and make your own judgment regarding its value in helping your presentation.

Taped Draft

A more effective method of providing feedback is to tape your presentation on cassette. Try to listen to the tape objectively. First, listen for the major areas of the presentation: the introduction, body, and close. Are they all there? Do they flow together smoothly? Do your key points stand out? Is the message persuasive? Once you are satisfied with the basic elements of your presentation, listen a bit more critically and try to address some of the items discussed in the next chapter:

- Did you have any verbal faults? Grammar? Pronunciation? "Ahs" and "ums"?
- Were your supporting data clear and convincing?
- Was your tone energetic and your enthusiasm for the topic apparent?
- Did you vary your rate of speech and fluctuation of pitch?
- Did you make an effective use of silence?
- Were you within time limits?

Do not be too critical of your presentation. Be sure to compliment yourself on the strengths of your presentation. If you can, videotape your presentation to provide even more feedback for your improvement. Your nonverbal behavior such as your gestures, facial expressions, and body movements can be analyzed using a videotape. Have another person give you a critique for either the audiotape or videotape. The added perspective will help you.

Live Audience Draft

Perhaps the best practice for your presentation will be to practice on other people. Having an informal audience, no matter what size or makeup, is a step closer to your speaking situation. First attempt your presentation with a member of your household and then with someone from your work environment.

Besides getting your audience members' critique, you will have the immediate feedback that comes from reading faces as you speak. When do they look puzzled? When are they smiling or laughing? Do any heads nod in agreement or disagreement? Before your practice session, give the detailed presentation evaluation form at the end of this chapter to members of your practice audience to help them constructively evaluate your presentation. Ask your audience members to watch specific areas in which you want feedback, or ask them pointed questions about your delivery when you are finished: Was I clear throughout? What was the vaguest area? Which points were most convincing and why? Did I convince you of my objective? If not, what more would you need to be convinced? Remember, the audience members can ask you questions during or after your practice presentation. What better way to anticipate the actual questions you are likely to receive?

STEP 3: MASTERING YOUR ACT

By this time you should be feeling quite confident about your presentation. To put the finishing touches on your practice, you should prepare and conduct a dress rehearsal of your presentation. Following are some ideas for polishing your presentation.

Practice the Rough Spots

After you have been through your presentation several times, try practicing just the rough spots. Try those areas, along with your opening and closing remarks, key points, and transitions until they are extremely comfortable. These areas of your presentation can be practiced during "transitional" time such as when you are in the shower or driving somewhere.

Practice with Revised Notes

As you put your outline to the practice test, you will probably want to make changes, deletions, and additions to your presentation. If your original notes become too cluttered with changes, you should rewrite them. If you rewrite your outline, always be sure to make a practice run using the new outline, or you may have trouble with it in your final presentation.

Use Your Actual Presentation Aids

During your last practice drafts, you should use whatever visual aids or handouts you plan on using during your presentation. Talk through each visual. This serves as the final check of whether you have too many visuals and identifies any that might be confusing.

Envision the Audience's Response

In your last few rehearsals, try to imagine how your audience is going to react to your presentation. Examine your analysis of the audience that you developed during the planning stage, and try to predict typical questions that the audience is likely to have. If you think of a question or objection that might detract from the persuasiveness of your presentation, then build that objection or information into your presentation. For example, say something like, "Some of you might be asking yourselves, If this is such a great idea, why we haven't done it already? Let me tell you why." You can turn an audience around by incorporating their doubts and objections into your presentation.

Make it a goal of your practice sessions to identify 10 of the most likely questions or objections you will get during your presentation. If you cannot come up with 10 questions or objections, then you are probably not anticipating all of the possible audience reactions to your presentation. It's better to anticipate questions that do not arise than it is to wish you had anticipated a question you cannot answer. In some companies the only advice passed down from senior management to those who are new to presenting is this: "Make sure you can answer any question you might get." You are going to win over your audience if you have thought through their objections or questions.

Do a Dress Rehearsal

As if for a play, plan to have a dress rehearsal for your final presentation. Schedule it for the same time of day in the same room. Wear the clothes you plan to have on for your presentation. Try to have at least a few of the members of the audience present. Without stopping, give your presentation and handle questions from the individuals. This activity should erase any lingering doubts you might have about your readiness. You really can't do anything better to prepare yourself for your presentation.

COMMONLY ASKED QUESTIONS

Maybe you really hadn't thought about practicing your presentation. Or maybe you had only planned on practicing your presentation once. Let's answer some questions you might have been asking yourself while you were reading this chapter.

1. *Isn't this a lot of practicing for a single presentation?* You're right—it is a lot practice. The amount of time that you spend practicing should vary with the difficulty of the original assignment. If you know the topic well and have presented it to the group before and are a fairly confident speaker,

many, if not most, of these practice steps can be skipped. These are only options for various degrees of presentation difficulty. Adapt them to your own style and schedule as needed. Keep in mind, however, that some experts suggest that the amount of time you practice should equal five times the length of your presentation. And, if you have any stage fright anxiety, most of it will be eliminated with adequate preparation.

2. *Can you practice too much?* Again, you are right—you can. If you practice to the point where the same wording comes from your mouth each time, you are probably overdoing it. You do not want to destroy any freshness or spontaneity in your delivery. Ideally, you want to be comfortable explaining your points a number of different ways, as you would if you were describing a picture. Only your introduction, transitions, and closing should be closer to a verbatim speech, but stay flexible.

3. *What if I don't have time to practice my presentation?* If this is your situation, join the majority of all speakers. We all have time constraints, but if the benefits of giving a professional presentation are important enough to you, perhaps some of your priorities can be rearranged to allow adequate preparation time. Prepare a preparation schedule for the time that you do have. For example, if you have a lunch break available, plan on going to a quiet place and mentally reviewing your presentation. Try to go over your presentation from start to finish at least one time before your actual presentation.

If you do not have a choice as to when you will accept a speaking engagement, you might try some other techniques for keeping your preparation on target. For example, try blocking out time on your schedule to specifically prepare for your presentation, as you would for a meeting. Use the planning sheet at the end of this chapter to establish deadlines for the different stages of your preparation. Include an adequate time buffer in case you fall behind. Finally, gain reassurance from knowing that each presentation will be that much easier, and, although none of the steps should be omitted altogether, you can spend a minimum amount of time on each stage as your level of expertise increases.

PRESENTATION PREPARATION AND PRACTICE SCHEDULE

Use this form to set up your schedule for preparing and practicing your presentation. Mark down the dates on your calendar and plan to stick to them.

Task	Completion Date
1. Plan my presentation.	
A. Write out the purpose of my presentation.	_____
B. Learn who my audience is going to be.	_____
C. Find out about the setting.	_____
D. Jot down and prioritize my ideas.	_____
2. Prepare my presentation.	
A. Outline the body of my presentation.	_____
B. Develop my supporting data for the presentation.	_____
C. Write my transitions between the main points of my presentation.	_____
D. Develop my introduction.	_____
E. Develop my conclusion.	_____
F. Prepare the notes for my presentation.	_____

Task	*Completion Date*

3. Develop visual aids.

   A. Complete rough drafts
      of visual aids.   _____

   B. Complete finished versions
      of visuals.   _____

4. Practice my presentation.
   A. Mental draft   _____

   B. Speaking draft   _____

   C. Standing draft   _____

   D. Mirrored draft   _____

   E. Taped draft   _____

   F. Live audience draft   _____

   G. Practice the rough spots _____

   H. Practice with revised notes _____

   I. Practice with visual aids _____

   J. Dress rehearsal   _____

DETAILED PRESENTATION EVALUATION FORM

Give this form to members of your audience when you practice your presentation. Part I includes a form for doing an overall evaluation of your speech. Parts II through VI include forms for evaluating different aspects of your presentation.

Presenter _____ Date _____

Presentation title _____

Audience _____ Location _____

Purpose _____

_____

I. Overall evaluation

Did the speaker achieve the intended purpose? Why or why not?

_____

_____

_____

_____

Effectiveness. Circle one: 1 = poor, 5 = excellent

Presentation	1	2	3	4	5	n/a
Speaker	1	2	3	4	5	n/a
Content	1	2	3	4	5	n/a

II. Presentation content

The left column lists different aspects of your presentation. For each item, have the audience check off phrases from the right column that best describe that aspect of your presentation.

A. Introduction
    1. Attention getter:
        Too brief _____
        Not attention getting _____
        Inappropriate _____
        Commanded my _____ attention

    2. Thesis:
        Missing _____
        Incomplete _____
        Unclear _____
        Clear and complete _____

    3. Significance statement:
        Missing _____
        Too short _____
        Too long _____
        Correct _____

    4. Overview:
        Missing _____
        Too short _____
        Too long _____
        Points not numbered _____
        Correct _____

    5. Transition:
        Missing _____
        Too short _____
        Too long _____
        Correct _____

B. Body
    1. Main points:
        Missing _____
        Unclear _____
        Too few _____
        Too many _____
        Appropriate _____

2. Organization: Missing _____

Unclear _____

Rambling _____

Clear _____

Logical _____

Effective _____

3. Supporting data: Missing _____

Scant _____

Ineffective _____

Adequate _____

Varied _____

Effective _____

4. Audiovisuals: Ineffective _____

Too many _____

Poorly designed _____

Too few _____

Effective _____

5. Transitions: Missing _____

Too short _____

Too long _____

Correct _____

C. Conclusion

1. Summary: Missing _____

Too brief _____

Too long _____

New information _____

Effective _____

2. Review: Missing _____

Ineffective _____

                                  Points not numbered _____
                                  Memorable _____

3. Action:
- Missing _____
- Unclear _____
- Excessive _____
- Attainable _____
- Motivating _____

4. Closing statement:
- Weak _____
- Ineffective _____
- Unplanned _____
- Clear _____
- Effective _____
- Strong _____

5. Fielding questions:
- Unprepared _____
- Rejects questions _____
- Too abrupt _____
- Vague _____
- Rambling _____
- Effective _____

III. Verbal delivery
  A. Personal qualities
    1. Enthusiasm:
- Missing _____
- Weak _____
- Unenergetic _____
- Exciting _____
- Contagious _____

    2. Empathy:
- Missing _____
- Uncaring _____
- Aloof _____

	Sympathetic	_____
	Sincere	_____
3. Personality:	Not showing	_____
	Stiff	_____
	Too formal	_____
	Personable	_____
	Likable	_____

B. Vocal qualities

  1. Volume:

- Too quiet _____
- Too loud _____
- No variety _____
- Correct _____

  2. Rate:

- Too slow _____
- Too fast _____
- No variety _____
- Good _____

  3. Pitch:

- Too high _____
- No variety _____
- Monotonous _____
- Varied and correct _____

  4. Word selection:

- Inappropriate _____
- Poor _____
- Heavy jargon _____
- Good _____
- Effective _____

  5. Pronunciation:

- Poor _____
- Highlights mistakes _____
- Correct _____

6. Enunciation: Mumbles _____
                       Sloppy _____
                       Closed mouth _____
                       Opened mouth _____
                       Clear _____
                       Precise _____

7. Tone: Abrasive _____
                       Hurried _____
                       Choppy _____
                       Soothing _____
                       Effective _____

8. Flaws: Excessive _____
                       Annoying _____
                       Emphasized _____
                       Minimal _____
                       Well handled _____
                       Unnoticed _____

C. Time
   Delivery time: Too long _____
                       Too short _____
                       On time _____

IV. Nonverbal delivery
    A. Dress: Inappropriate _____
                       Too casual _____
                       Too formal _____
                       Appropriate _____

    B. Smile: Missing _____
                       Nervous _____
                       Present _____
                       Natural _____

C. Eye contact: Scant _____
                       Fleeting _____
                       Limited _____
                       Appropriate _____
                       Extensive _____

D. Posture: Poor _____
                       Sloppy _____
                       Rigid _____
                       Shifting _____
                       Excessive movement _____
                       Erect _____

E. Gestures: Missing _____
                       Limited _____
                       Forced _____
                       Natural _____
                       Appropriate _____
                       Dynamic _____

F. Mannerisms: Excessive _____
                       Uncontrolled _____
                       Limited _____
                       Unnoticed _____

V. Communicative techniques
   A. Audience   Over their heads _____
      involvement: Marginally interested _____
                       Involved _____
                       Excited _____

   B. Clarity: Confusing _____
                       Vague and rambling _____
                       Numbered points _____
                       Clear organization _____

C. Humor: Inappropriate _____
                         Excessive _____
                         Ineffective _____
                         Appropriate _____
                         Effective _____

D. Logical appeal: Poor arguments _____
                         Too few _____
                         Good arguments _____

E. Psychological   Focused on needs
   appeal: of speaker _____
                         Focused on needs of some
                         audience members _____
                         Focused on needs of all
                         audience members _____

F. Personal appeal: Nervous _____
                         Evasive _____
                         Authoritarian _____
                         Aloof _____
                         Defensive _____
                         Confused _____
                         Trustworthy _____
                         Confident _____
                         Positive _____
                         Persuasive _____

G. Emotional   Inappropriate _____
   appeal: Unmotivating _____
                         Dynamic _____
                         Persuasive _____

Please write any additional comments below.

Chapter Seven

Refining Your Style

How you deliver your message is just as important as what it is. This chapter examines techniques for improving both your verbal and nonverbal communication with the audience. Your nonverbal communication is just as important as your verbal communication. Experts agree that your nonverbal behavior represents 60 to 90 percent of everything you communicate. Your audience decides whether it trusts you based on your nonverbal signals. Following are some suggestions for improving both your verbal and nonverbal communication during a presentation.

TECHNIQUES OF GOOD VERBAL COMMUNICATION

Strive for a Conversational Tone

Normal conversation should be the model for both your verbal and nonverbal communication during a presentation. People usually speak more directly and with more animation in conversation than when delivering a presentation to a group. Observe yourself when you are talking to a friend—note your gestures and your methods for explaining topics. Try to use some of these techniques during your presentation. Think of your presentation as a one-way conversation in which you state your points in clear, direct language. Continue to your next point when you perceive that your audience understands your point. You can sense when the audience members understand your point from the looks on their faces and the nodding of their heads. If you have trouble making your delivery conversational, invite a friend to your practice and give your presentation to your friend. All your practices should be in the first person.

Emphasize Your Organization

Frequently let your audience know where you are in your presentation and where you are headed. Repeat your organization and main points to help your audience remember your main ideas. If your main points are organized in a way that is logical or catchy, refer to the organization even more: "I want us to STOP what we are doing. That is, to STructure the Organization's Priorities before additional resources are wasted. I think we should STOP now, and I'll tell you why." In this case, an acronym helps clarify the organization.

Show Enthusiasm

Show enthusiasm for your topic. Enthusiasm makes up for a number of other deficiencies that you might have in your presentation. Your enthusiasm for your topic, the situation, and the audience helps create interest in what you have to say and motivates your audience to act on it. The external indicators of an enthusiastic delivery include a clear, strong voice, crisp pace, and vocal emphasis. Enthusiasm is difficult to fake if you are not really excited about your presentation, so try to communicate only messages that you really believe in. Otherwise, give a different message or convince yourself that what you have to communicate is important, necessary, or both. If you do not, your enthusiasm might seem phony to the audience.

Show Your Personality

As you become more experienced and comfortable with public speaking, more and more of your personality will come through in what you say. Personality comes through in the manner in which you speak. Your personality is demonstrated in the way you word your ideas and in the ideas you choose to share. If you interject personal examples—even if they are embarrassing or show a mistake you made—or side comments, as you would in daily conversations, your presentational style will contain more personality.

Control Your Volume

If you can't be heard, you can't be persuasive. If you have any doubt as to whether your audience can hear you, ask when you begin your presentation. If you need to be louder, use greater force in your voice coupled with the support of a larger column of air. Practice speaking in an empty room—speak so that someone can hear you at the extreme corners of the room. Even if you are small and quiet, you can learn to increase your volume without feeling like you are straining your voice.

Vary your volume to control your audience. Speak louder and slower during key phrases in the opening, main points, transitions, and conclusions. Increasing your volume adds emphasis to what you are saying. You can also attract the attention of the audience by reducing your volume—everybody wants to know what you are whispering. Try bringing your voice to just above a whisper and you will find that most groups become more attentive. This technique is used by many professional speakers to draw the audience to the speaker and to have it hanging on to each and every word that the speaker emits. It is a good technique to use when a group gets too noisy in a discussion.

Control Your Speaking Rate

You should vary your speaking rate. People usually understand words spoken at a rate of up to four times faster than
typical conversation, so don't be afraid of going too fast. If
you are speaking quickly, make sure that you occasionally
slow down. It is also important not to speak too slowly. If
you speak too slowly, your audience will either tune out or
lose its patience. The best thing to do is to vary your rate,
speaking faster when less important information is being
communicated and more slowly to emphasize information.
Or focus on interjecting pauses during a faster delivery to
highlight your main points. Either method alerts the audience that you are moving to a new point or emphasizing a
point.

Select Your Words Carefully

Make your language appropriate to the situation and group
you are addressing. The most common mistake people make
is to use words that are not familiar to the audience. If you
use a term that is specific for your topic or industry, define
it if you suspect that a member of the audience does not
understand the word, or use a more commonly known term
to explain the same point. Avoid slang or inappropriate
language, including swearing. Some speakers will swear to
give emphasis to their points or to display their power, but
this is seldom necessary to achieve your goals.

Enunciate

Pronounce your words clearly and distinctly, so that they
are properly understood. The most common enunciation
mistakes include dropping the endings of words such as

comin', hopin', meetin'; slurring your speech; mumbling words; speaking with your mouth half closed; and trailing off the endings of sentences. Audiences are quickly turned off by poor, sloppy, and inarticulate diction.

Poor enunciation can be corrected by increasing the amount of energy to your lips, mouth, and jaw and controlling the muscles in those areas with more precision. Many speakers repeat the vowels over and over again on their way to giving a presentation. With each time through, they vary the emphasis, muscle movement, and rate of speaking until they feel confident that their mouth is warmed up. The same drill can be done with the entire alphabet or with tongue twisters. With each, open your mouth as wide as possible and exaggerate all movements. Drills like these have been known to produce a noticeable improvement in only a week or two when practiced every day. Or you may want to try what ancient Greek orators tried when poor diction was a problem: Speak while your mouth is full of pebbles.

Watch for Repeated Words

Speakers commonly repeat words over and over at the beginning or end of sentences; *also, and, next, so,* and *well* are the biggest offenders. This repetition draws attention away from the topic and audience members may start counting the times the word is used. Avoid these errors by learning to become comfortable with silence. You do not always have to be saying something; your speech will be more effective if you pause when you are mentally grabbing for your next words. Practicing pauses when you practice your presentation will help. Writing the verbal crutch in large letters in the margin of your notes helps you avoid it during delivery. Once you catch yourself using these unnecessary words, you will be well on the way to eliminating them.

TECHNIQUES OF GOOD NONVERBAL COMMUNICATION

Don't Forget to Smile

One of the most effective means of projecting a confident image, increasing trust, and getting your audience to like you is to smile. Smiling is one of the few universal signs of communication. Using a smile will help put your audience at ease and make your message more convincing.

Use Eye Contact

Even more important than smiling is the quality and quantity of your eye contact. Eye contact is closely linked with your sincerity. One study attributes 38 percent of all meaning that an audience perceives to the eye contact of the speaker. Your eye contact should be steady, not fleeting from side to side or up and down. You should focus on each member of the audience several times in the course of your presentation. Finally, you should avoid looking excessively at your notes, at the floor or ceiling, or out a window or door.

One effective technique that is easily incorporated into your delivery style is to look an individual member of the audience in the eye until you have completed your thought and then move on to another person. With practice, this technique makes for a very smooth delivery style that lets the audience feel as though you are communicating in a very personal manner, and it makes you feel more at ease because you are talking with individuals. By using eye contact with your audience, you are signaling to them that you consider them friends.

Use Gestures

Gestures add emphasis to your points and keep your audience interested in what you have to say. Some gestures may

Smile and look audience members in the eye.

seem unnatural or forced to a novice speaker, but they are an effective tool for a presentation. Arm movements, head nods, and facial expressions are all examples of gestures you should be using. They are easily incorporated by observing which gestures you use in one-on-one conversation and simply amplifying those same movements for a group situation. Another technique is to "break" the space around you when you are practicing your delivery by swinging your arms and stretching them over your head. Then try to incorporate that same range of movement into your practice presentations: pointing, holding arms out, numbering points with your fingers, covering your head, and so on. Several will seem more natural for you and those are the ones you should use extensively. Don't practice or plan specific gestures for making specific points because this will appear staged and lose its effectiveness. Instead, practice gesturing, in general. You'll find that gesturing also provides an excellent release for nervous energy.

Walk Around

Walking is an effective way for controlling the attention of the group. Move closer to individuals whose interest you are losing, or move away from the front of the room to encourage audience discussion. If appropriate, you can come across as more casual while relaxing yourself by walking in front of the lectern and sitting on the edge of a table as you speak. What you want to avoid is walking in a set pattern. If you do this, your movement will be distracting to the group.

TECHNIQUES OF CONTROLLING THE AUDIENCE

Speak with the Audience

You keep the audience more interested if you talk with it and not at it. You have to develop a sense for when the audience is with you and when it is not. Watch for clues from members' facial expressions, eyes, and nonverbal behavior. If they look like they are about to fall asleep, you probably are not getting through. Experienced speakers, at times, talk about the concept of having the audience with you by using the analogy of a wave. Your thoughts and ideas flow out over the audience, and you draw back a response to your words. If you find uncertainty in the audience's response, you need to present the same information in a different way (a story, example, more data) until the message is clear to the group. Imagine that you are speaking *for* the group as you speak *to* it.

Avoid Rambling

As you describe your points, be sure not to overelaborate on them. You will lose your audience. Once you sense that the audience understands your point, do not continue to give another example. Do not distribute a handout and then proceed to read the information from the handout to the group. This kind of behavior insults your audience and should be avoided.

Regain Their Attention

Don't let it get to you if the audience's attention drifts during your presentation. Just do something different and unexpected. Ask a question or ask for questions, change your location in the room, or take a brief break, if appropriate. Another trick is to use the names of individuals in the group: "Now, John, I know you're probably saying. . ." or "Jackie has told me on several occasions that the department could expand operations if it were to . . ."

Show Empathy

An important factor is your empathy for your audience. Empathy is the amount of care you have for the audience: your concern for understanding them, wanting them to hear what you have to say, answering their questions, and generally helping them in whatever capacity that is possible as a speaker. Like enthusiasm, it is difficult to fake, and perhaps even harder to develop if it does not exist. You must convince yourself that members of the audience are truly interested in what you have to say. Try to imagine what it's like to be sitting in their seats listening to your presentation. Try to see things from the audience's perspective.

CHECKLIST TO REFINE YOUR STYLE

Check off the items on the following list that you want to work on. Then run through another practice of your presentation and try out some of the things you have checked off.

1. Techniques of good verbal communication:

    A. Use conversational tone.   _____

    B. Emphasize your organization.   _____

    C. Show enthusiasm.   _____

    D. Show your personality.   _____

    E. Control your volume.   _____

    F. Control your speaking rate.   _____

    G. Select your words carefully.   _____

    H. Enunciate.   _____

    I. Watch for repeated words.   _____

2. Techniques of good nonverbal communication:

    A. Don't forget to smile.   _____

    B. Use eye contact.   _____

    C. Use gestures.   _____

    D. Walk around.   _____

3. Techniques of controlling the audience:

    A. Speak with, not at, the audience.   _____

    B. Avoid rambling.   _____

    C. Regain the audience's attention.   _____

    D. Show empathy.   _____

Chapter Eight

On the Day of Your Presentation

When the day of your presentation arrives, you should act and think differently to help mentally psyche yourself up for the approaching event. Let's consider the time period from your awakening on the day of your presentation to the moment when the announcer introduces you as the next speaker.

STAYING CONFIDENT ON THE MORNING OF YOUR PRESENTATION

No matter how many times you've practiced, you may start losing some of your confidence when the day of your presentation arrives. Let's look at some tricks for keeping your confidence up.

Greet the Day with Anticipation

It may seem corny, but try springing out of bed and saying, "My big day!" rather than groaning and rolling over to escape reality for a few more moments. This helps set the tone for the day. You need to be up for a quality delivery, and this is easier if you begin the day at an energetic level. Thinking and saying positive statements to yourself affect your mental disposition and level of confidence. Make up statements that you are comfortable with, or choose from these examples:

- "I really feel prepared for this presentation; I'm glad I'm doing it."
- "That audience is going to be impressed. They are going to learn a lot they don't know."
- "This presentation should actually be fun. I'm planning to enjoy giving it."

Do Something Special

Another way to make yourself feel mentally and physically better is treat yourself specially during the day. Make a small purchase of an item—perhaps on a whim as you see something you like in a store. Have favorite foods for breakfast or lunch. Call a friend you haven't spoken with for some time. Compliment a co-worker on his or her work or appearance. Any positive activity that you do out of the ordinary will more than likely have a positive effect on you.

Go through One More Practice

Even if you have practiced your presentation a thousand times before, it helps your confidence to practice one more time on the day of your presentation. The practice can be as simple as running through your presentation in your head, but you'll find that it is worth the time and effort.

Wear Favorite Clothes

As long as it is appropriate to the speaking situation, choose an outfit you feel comfortable in for your presentation. Your dress should be a notch nicer than that of your audience. When in doubt, dress more formally to show that you have respect for the situation, the audience, and your position as a speaker. Avoid any sharp changes in your appearance such as a haircut on the day of your presentation; you might feel too self-conscious.

Arrive Early

Plan to be at the place of your presentation at least an hour before the audience's arrival. Come even earlier if you have a variety of equipment to check. Use the checklist at the end of this chapter to check all the preliminary arrangements. To make it just a little more familiar and comfortable for you when you begin, spend a few moments at the lectern or spot from which you will be speaking.

Check Your Introduction

Talk with the person who will be introducing you to check whether he or she has enough information about you and the topic. Make suggestions as to what information might enhance your credibility or build the interest of your audience.

JUST BEFORE YOU SPEAK

When you are called on to speak, you enter a different world. Even though it may seem unfamiliar at first, facing a group may be one of the most rewarding experiences you will ever have.

Relax while You Wait

If there are speakers or other agenda items before your presentation, focus your attention on staying relaxed. Take slow deep breaths and stretch any muscles that start to become tight. Avoid thinking about your speech's content other than the words you plan to begin with. If you are relaxed, focus on the other activities going on in the room.

Don't Make Any Changes

Avoid any tendency to make last minute changes or "improvements" to your presentation, especially in your introductory remarks. Changes at this stage are apt to confuse you and possibly throw off your delivery. This rule does not include a spontaneous introduction that is an extension of your introducer's remarks. If you think of a good spontaneous introduction that fits the situation, go ahead and use it.

Listen Closely to Your Introduction

Listen while you are being introduced to check whether you will need to add to or correct what the audience is being told about you. This is important because it is likely that many people in your audience do not know you. What they hear from your introduction will set their expectations of you.

Spring from Your Seat

Get the attention of your audience in a direct, aggressive way by snapping out of your seat and briskly approaching the lectern. The confidence and authority you will emit will enhance your credibility. Your energy level will be contagious.

Greet the Audience

If you are up at the podium waiting for audience members to enter the room (say, at a conference), from the moment the first audience member enters the room pretend you are on stage. Act as though all attention is focused on you, even when it is not. By taking this perspective, when all attention does come to be focused on you in a short while, it will not seem so disruptive to you. Try to establish physical contact and individually meet each member of the audience before your presentation. The purpose is to increase their familiarity with you. Your initial contact also helps dispel any possible hostility from group members. People tend to be less critical of those they know and like, and your initial contact can help to establish that rapport.

Minimize Prespeech Activities

Your visual aids should all be in place and set to go. Ideally, you should have your notes already placed at the lectern in a stiff folder, or carry such a folder up with you. Avoid having to hunt for and unfold notes taken from your pocket. If there is no lectern, keep your notes in your hand or on a nearby table. Avoid having to move objects or the lectern to a different location. Such activities only distract from your presentation. If you need to make a change, do so before you say anything, or you might end up fumbling with a microphone for several minutes into your presentation.

Wait for the Audience's Attention

Many speakers, especially if they are nervous, prefer to charge right into their presentation, even if the group is not listening to them. Avoid this tendency. Instead, look at the audience from side to side and wait for all to be looking at you. If several members of the group are chatting, they will quickly stop when they observe that you are looking at them.

Pause and Begin

When you have the attention of the group, start your presentation in a loud, clear voice, using the exact wording that

Wait for the audience's attention before you begin.

you practiced and focused on while you were seated. You should not have to glance at your notes to begin speaking, especially if your opening remark is a phrase such as, "It's a pleasure to be here." Do not begin with an apology of any type, especially for not being prepared.

PRELIMINARY ARRANGEMENTS CHECKLIST

Go through this planning sheet on the day of your presentation to make sure that everything is in order when you go to deliver your presentation.

Session: _____

Date and time: _____ Room: _____ No. expected ____

Seating arrangement:

Auditorium _____ Classroom _____

Informal _____ U-Shape _____

Other _____

Room and supplies:

Satisfactory   Not needed   Needs attention

Chairs _____

Tables _____

Lighting _____

Ventilation _____

Distractions _____

Ash trays _____

Pencils, scratch paper _____

Name cards _____

Coffee, soft drinks, water _____

_____

_____

Handouts _____

_____

_____

_____

Electrical accessories (bulb, cord, plug, extension) _____

_____

_____

Audiovisual equipment _____

_____

Supplies (chalk, eraser, felt pens, grease pencil, tape)

_____

_____

_____

Audience notification _____

_____

Chapter Nine

Special Speaking Situations

This chapter discusses some special speaking situations you might encounter during your professional career. In particular, this chapter describes how to deal with a hostile audience, how to give an impromptu presentation, and how to introduce another speaker. It also includes some suggestions for using humor in your presentation and for responding to questions from the audience.

HANDLING A HOSTILE AUDIENCE

It is important to be prepared for an audience that is hostile toward you, your topic, or the situation. Hopefully, you can predict some of the hostilities ahead of time through your audience analysis. If you anticipate hostilities ahead of time, you should be able to work some of their objections into your presentation. Try some of the following techniques if you find yourself in front of a hostile group.

Clarify the Hostility

As soon as you detect any hostility, try to determine why it is there. If possible, ask the person who made a hostile comment for further explanation of his or her viewpoint.

Otherwise, you may inadvertently continue to offend members of the audience or alienate yourself from them.

Emphasize the Similarities

Try to identify and expand the points of mutual agreement between you and those who disagree with what you are saying. Focus on how the two sides are similar. Emphasize how much you are like them in whatever ways this might be true.

Work Objections into Your Presentation

If you are reasonably sure that an objection will be brought up by members of the audience, bring it up first in your presentation. "Now I know there are those present who disagree with the planned proposal. I understand that position and hope they will understand why this proposal *will* benefit their cause. Specifically, there are three reasons . . ." Or, better yet, directly cut off an objection by stating: "There is one possible objection that I want to answer right now so that no one will bring it up when I'm finished. It concerns the phase-in period . . ." It would take an especially gutsy audience member to later bring up the same objection. Other members of the audience are likely to think, Wasn't that guy listening?

Don't Get Personal

If you do get into an argument, focus on the topic, not the person. Avoid responding to emotional outbreaks or personal jabs at your character. Remember that you have the higher level of authority as a speaker in this situation. You will lose credibility in the situation if you stoop to an unprofessional level.

Use Humor as a Release

An appropriate joke can help relieve pressure for you and the audience. Do not, however, use humor to discount the audience's concerns or make a joke at their expense.

Admit It when You Are Wrong

If at all possible, admit to an error when you make a mistake and a member of the audience corrects you. Your honest, open attitude will gain you support from other members of the audience, and you will gain credibility when you do stand your ground.

GIVING IMPROMPTU PRESENTATIONS

Sometimes you will have little or no warning that you will be called on to speak. It is a scary situation even for experienced speakers because you probably are not prepared, and you might not even be an expert on the topic that you are called on to discuss. Let's look at how to make impromptu presentations easier to handle.

Prepare for It

Although there are several unknowns in an impromptu speaking situation, it is still possible to prepare for one. First, try to predict when you might be called on. Often, if others know that you are knowledgeable about a topic, they are likely to ask your opinion. For example, if you are going to a staff meeting in which one of the agenda items is next year's budget, and you have been collecting data on that topic, it is a safe bet that you will be asked to contribute to the conversation. Or, if you are an avid runner and the group you are in starts talking about physical fitness, it is likely that you will be asked about your beliefs and practices.

Fortunately, in most situations in which you are asked to speak without warning, it is because someone else believes you are knowledgeable on the topic. Even if you are not, you will seldom be asked for facts and figures, but rather for opinions and ideas—and it is possible to have an opinion about anything.

Another technique for preparing is to always have some stories or speaking strategies ready. Save the notes from previous presentations, and abbreviate the information, or carry a trinket that can easily be converted into a story. An example of this latter point is this: Some professional speakers carry a coin that has a favorite saying or motto on it that is applicable to a wide range of topics, a quotation about trust, for example. When called on to speak, they begin with the quote and a display of the coin and then explain how the topic is relevant to the present situation. Their stock, but impressive, opening gives them a few extra minutes to determine what to say next.

A similar approach is to begin an impromptu talk with a personal story that recently occurred, perhaps that same morning. Then, as you are speaking, determine how you can twist your story to apply it to the topic at hand. This may seem difficult, but with some practice you can quickly become skilled. Following are two impromptu organization formats that can be adapted to nearly every situation.

Take a Stand and Defend It

As you are rising to speak, grab onto the first logical idea that crosses your mind, pause once you are standing, and begin with a clear, specific stand on the topic. Support your contention with any of the suggestions given earlier in this book, such as a story, something you read in the newspaper, or something you heard from a friend. After you have backed up your claim with two or three bits of support, come full circle, repeat your initial position, and sit down. Some individuals believe that if you start a talk and end a talk in a decisive or clever manner (such as returning to the same story you began with and adding a new twist), it doesn't matter what you say in between.

Past, Present, and Future

The other standard format that you can usually count on for an effective impromptu presentation is to organize your information in a chronological manner. Start with the past: how the situation being discussed has come about. Explain the present: what is being done now. And offer a plan for the future: what should be done to correct, resolve, or change the situation. This format can also be applied to the speaking situation itself: what you have to say on the topic, and what others there should think about the topic.

Once you overcome any shyness for impromptu speaking, you need to be careful not to abuse the privilege that comes with this opportunity. Speakers often ramble, get off the subject, or needlessly repeat themselves. When you have completed what you have to say, sit down.

INTRODUCING A SPEAKER

You will probably come across the opportunity to introduce another speaker. This task does not sound very intimidating, yet very few people are skilled at this relatively simple assignment. A good introduction incorporates the following steps.

Welcome and Introduction

You have the responsibility of warming up the audience for the speaker. You should first welcome the group and take a moment to establish a rapport with the audience. Then discuss the purpose of the meeting, the topic of the presentation, and the reasons why that topic is important and relevant. Often a speaker will write his or her own introduction and will want it read, as is, without any changes. A good introduction for a speaker should include the following elements.

Speaker's Qualifications

Without mentioning his or her name, mention the speaker's outstanding qualifications for presenting information on the topic. Build the audience's anticipation and excitement for the speaker. Give the speaker's qualifications a personal touch if possible. Mention what you know about the speaker, or a personal experience that you had with him or her.

Speaker's Name and Title

When the audience's interest is at a peak, conclude your introduction with the name of the presenter and the title of his or her presentation. "Help me welcome _____ , who is speaking to us today on _____ ." Lead the applause and continue it until the speaker reaches the front of the room. Shake hands with the speaker and leave the front of the room on the opposite side that he or she arrived on; that is, do not cross in front of or in back of the speaker.

USING HUMOR

Humor facilitates a great delivery when used correctly. It lifts spirits, attracts attention, releases tension, and gets people to like you. Unfortunately, humor is often misused by presenters. Speakers often cut down their own jokes, use inappropriate humor for the occasion, or end up just not being funny. The secret to being funny is developing your own style, learning a few tricks, and taking the time to practice.

Build a Collection of Humor

Search for jokes and stories on a regular basis. Jot down these jokes, asides, and stories that you think are funny. Review your collection to discover your own taste. Figure out whether you are better delivering stories or one-liners. Magazines, newspapers, and personal experiences with your family are all good sources of humor.

Let the Audience Members Know when They Are Supposed to Laugh

Many times an audience is not sure when to laugh. No one wants to laugh at a statement that was meant to be serious. If you have a dry wit or a believably sarcastic tone, you may leave the audience members guessing as to whether or not they are supposed to laugh. Be careful if you introduce humor for the first time late in your speech. The audience will probably not be expecting you to be funny and most likely will miss the humor. You can subtly introduce your humor with a disclaimer such as, "A funny thing happened as I was preparing this presentation . . ." or, "An example will make my point clear in a humorous way . . ."

Be Sure Your Humor Is Funny and Appropriate

Use humor that you have heard work in other presentational settings, or test it on a group of co-workers. It needs to be appropriate for the situation and the audience. Inappropriate humor includes sexist and racist jokes. Also be careful with insult humor. When in doubt, leave it out.

Tie Your Humor to the Content of Your Presentation

It is important to connect your humor to the rest of your presentation; otherwise it will appear as though you are just making random jokes. You can do this by using a clever transition from the joke to your content such as, "That joke may seem funny, but our topic today is not . . ." or, "You might be as surprised as that person in the joke before I have finished today because I have some startling facts to give you."

A second way to tie humor to your content is called "pulling a switch" by comedians and comedy writers. With this method you take a joke and change the character, subject, setting, or all three to make the humor more relevant to the speaking situation. Let's examine an example. Suppose you have a line such as, "Finishing school is where you learn how to say 'fantastic' instead of 'baloney.' "You start your presentation by making the person who introduced you the "character" of this joke.

> I showed John some of my notes on what I planned to say today and he kept repeating "fantastic, fantastic, fantastic." I finally asked him if it was really good and he told me . . .

Or you can apply it to the subject of the presentation:

> I showed my manager the policy changes we'll be discussing today, and all she could say was "fantastic."

Or the setting may be changed:

> We've dealt with the customer. I followed one sales representative on his rounds last week and was impressed at how positive he always was. Regardless of what business we were at, or who he was speaking to, he kept interjecting

the word "fantastic" into the conversation. Finally, at the end of the day I asked him . . .

Humor can be a powerful tool for controlling the speaking situation. Learn its subtleties and you will be very fortunate. Pay attention to others who are funny to see what specifically it is they are doing. Practice your jokes over and over while varying your emphasis, timing, and gestures to see what works best.

HANDLING QUESTIONS

Most presentational situations allow members of the audience to ask questions. Good answers to the audience's questions enhance the effectiveness of your speech. If you handle yourself with authority and confidence, the audience will remain convinced of your message. Questions are an excellent opportunity for you to show your expertise on a subject. If, however, you become uneasy or ineffective (or worse, both) in answering straightforward questions about the topic, the entire effectiveness of your presentation may be in jeopardy. At this time you can tailor your message to the specific needs of individuals in the audience. In order to come across as professionally as possible, use the following guidelines when answering questions.

Repeat or Rephrase the Question

Repeating the question gives you a chance to organize your thoughts and make sure you clearly understand the question. It is also a courtesy to members of the audience who may not have heard the question. An example is, "Your question then is, How significantly will our forecasts be affected? Is that right?"

Don't get defensive when answering questions. Handle questions with authority and confidence.

Compliment the Tough Questions

Everyone likes to be flattered, and to give flattery in a speaking situation helps get individual audience members on your side. Complimenting the question also helps defuse any potential hostilities that the person asking the question might have. Be careful not to compliment every question—you will seem insincere if you do so. For example, "That is a relevant question, which brings up an important consideration."

Frame Your Answer

Qualify your response so that it does not contradict any other information you have already presented. If the question raises other concerns that you believe are relevant, discuss those topics as well, but be sure not to drift too far from the original question, or you might forget to answer it. An example is, "The best I can tell you given the data we have available is . . ."

Answer the Question Clearly

Make sure that you specifically address the individual's question. If, for example, it was a yes or no question, be sure to specifically answer yes or no, regardless of whatever additional information you use to buffer your answer. If you don't know. . . say so, but offer to find out. Answer a question whenever possible, but don't bluff information you are not sure about. For example, "That's an excellent question, which I don't have an answer to. I could find out, however, and get back to you later today."

Check the Clarity of Your Answers

If you have any doubts at all as to whether you answered a question satisfactorily, make sure you ask, "Did that answer your question?"

Keep Control of the Presentation

Constantly serve as the gatekeeper during question-and-answer periods, monitoring the length of questions and replies and the amount of interaction that takes place between audience members. For example, if an individual disagrees with your reply and proceeds to argue with you, interrupt him or her. Offer to discuss the topic further after the group adjourns, or state, "Let's try to get as many questions as possible. I see a few more hands, so let's hear from some others right now." You should also cut off and summarize people in the audience who start to ramble.

Your attitude about the audience's questions will in part determine how well you do answering their questions. If you view the audience's questions as though someone is trying to put you on the spot, then you are bound to become defensive with your answers. If you approach the audience's questions instead as an indicator that the audience is interested in what you have said and wants further clarification, then your time spent answering their questions will serve as a way to sell your audience on your ideas.

CHECKLIST FOR INTRODUCING A SPEAKER

1. Welcome
   A. Welcome the group.
   B. Establish rapport with the group.
   C. Discuss the purpose of the meeting.
   D. Introduce topic of the presentation and the reasons why it is relevant.
2. Speaker's qualifications
   Build up the audience's interest by discussing the speaker's qualifications without letting the audience know who the speaker is.
3. Speaker's name and title
   A. Introduce speaker's name and title.
   B. Lead the applause for the speaker.

CHECKLIST FOR IMPROMPTU PRESENTATIONS

1. Be ready for anything.
   A. Try to predict when you will be called on to speak.
   B. Always have some stories or speaking strategies ready.
2. Option 1: take a stand and defend it.
   A. Grab onto the first logical idea that crosses your mind.
   B. Pause when you are standing, and begin with a clear and specific stand on the topic.
   C. Support your contention with a story, something you read in the newspaper, or something you heard from a friend.

    D. After you have backed up your claim with two or three bits of support, come full circle, repeat your initial position, and sit down.

3. Option 2: past, present, and future.

    A. Start with the past and discuss how the situation has come about.

    B. Explain the present and discuss what is being done now.

    C. Offer a plan for the future: what should be done to correct or change the situation.

Chapter Ten

Learning from Experience

Without fail you will remember, the minute you sit down, something else you meant to say. Don't let it concern you. Most of us feel as though we could have done better in a presentation, and we can usually identify several factors that would have made a higher-quality presentation such as more practice, more information, more time, and so on and so forth ad infinitum. The fact of the matter is that all speakers are faced with those same constraints and to bring them up before, during, or after your presentation will just seem like excuses to members of your audience. Avoid using any kind of excuse during your presentation: "We've been under a lot of pressure, so I'm glad I was even able to pull this together."

GETTING REACTIONS

Now it is time to give yourself some feedback. You should first analyze your reactions to your presentation, and then the audience's reaction.

What Did You Think?

Perhaps the best evaluation of a presentation is made by the presenter. As the presenter, you know best what obstacles were present. Before you analyze any of the reactions from other people, try to identify a few items that you felt went exceedingly well and a few that could have gone better. This initial evaluation serves as a basis for gathering more feedback from others.

What Did Your Audience Think?

As you speak with members of the audience, you will probably find that most of the comments you receive will be positive. Accept those comments with gratitude, but press for a more detailed reaction to what could have been better. The point is that every presentation can be improved, and if you don't find out how your presentation can be improved, chances are that you will not do better the next time. If you know some of the members of the audience, have them complete an evaluation form such as the one included at the end of this chapter. This might give you some specific ideas as to how you can improve.

Did You Achieve Your Purpose?

Usually any reaction at the end of a presentation is referred to as a "happiness rating." You will receive only general comments about how good a job it was that you did and how pleased the members of the audience are with what they heard. Usually it is worthwhile to get a more thorough evaluation that examines what actually changed as a result of your presentation. Will members of the audience think or act differently as a result of your presentation? Did you achieve your purpose? These questions are not always easy to answer. Behavior changes will not be noticeable until the next opportunity for the audience member to act on the topic. For example, if your presentation was on changes in office procedures, you may not know whether the group members understood and will follow the changes until they have an opportunity to do so. Perhaps they indicated that they understood, but when the time comes to use what they learned, they are confused. Perhaps they will remember exactly what it is. They might then ask someone else in the department to see you for clarification. If your goal was to keep everyone in the department from coming to you for an explanation of the new procedure, your goal might only have been partially reached. If, however, you were primarily seeking to have members of the department stop using the old procedure, regardless of how they obtained information about the change, your presentation can be viewed as more successful.

MAKING CHANGES BASED ON YOUR EVALUATIONS

Let's now look at how you are going to improve your next presentation. Read the following sections, and write down a list of things you did right and a list of things you would like to do differently. File your list for your next presentation.

What Would You Do Differently?

If you were to give the same presentation again (which is possible), what would you do differently? What exactly have you learned, based on this experience? Unless you follow up on answers to these questions, you will not be the most effective speaker you can be. That is, your style will stagnate, and, although giving presentations may become easier for you, you will not become a better speaker. Make a list of the specific changes you will make in the preparation and delivery of your next presentation.

What Presentational Skills Do You Want to Develop?

In addition to the specific changes you plan to make for your next presentation, consider how you would like to generally improve as a speaker. Perhaps you might like to develop a stronger voice, make better use of humor, use more and better quotations, or focus on being more enthusiastic and dynamic. Select one or two areas for your general development, and develop a strategy for improvement. Your strategy might include joining a speaker's group such as Toastmasters International, obtaining additional speaking references such as a joke book, or practicing specific speaking skills such as articulation exercises. Set estimated time frames for each goal to increase your commitment to achieving each one.

Practice, Practice, Practice

Once you know the rules and have a satisfactory formula for giving a presentation, you need only practice to become an accomplished speaker. Look for opportunities to use your skills, no matter how formal or informal they might be. Speak up at social meetings, in your family setting, at staff meetings, even in elevators or on the bus. Come to relish the opportunity to say a few words when presented with a formal opportunity to speak. When asked, "Would you be willing to speak to our staff about . . ." learn to automatically respond, "I'd love to!" With that attitude, it is only a short time until you will be a truly professional speaker.

ABBREVIATED PRESENTATION EVALUATION FORM

Presenter _____ Date _____

Presentation title _____

Audience _____ Location _____

Purpose_____

_____

1. Did the speaker achieve the intended purpose? Why or why not?

2. What was best about the presentation?

3. What could have been improved in the presentation?

4. What were the speaker's best presentational qualities?

5. What presentational skills could the speaker improve on?

6. What did you learn from the presentation?

7. What will you do differently as a result of hearing
   this presentation?

Index

1. How did you find out about this Briefcase Book?

- [ ] Bookstore
- [ ] Advertisement
- [ ] Flyer
- [ ] Sales Rep
- [ ] Irwin Catalog
- [ ] Convention
- [ ] Other Catalog

other _____

2. Was this book provided by your organization or did you purchase this book for yourself?

- [ ] individual purchase
- [ ] organizational purchase

3. Are you using this book as a part of a training program?

- [ ] yes [ ] no

4. Did this book meet your expectations?

- [ ] yes [ ] no

(please explain) _____
_____
_____
_____

5. What other topics would you like to see addressed in this series?

(Please list)

_____
_____
_____

6. [ ] Please have a sales representative call me.

I am interested in:

- [ ] bulk purchase discounts
- [ ] custom publishing

7. [ ] Please send me a catalog of your products.

Name _____

Title _____

Organization _____

Address _____

City, State, Zip _____

Phone _____